My Wife By God's Decree

Sixteen Assumptions About Your Marriage That Change Everything

Michael K. Pasque
Email: pasquem@skyfiremusic.com

Chapter 1

By God's Holy Decree

Assumption # 1
Before a single atom was created, before a second of time had passed, God chose her specifically for you.

At one time or another, almost every one of us has favorably acknowledged God's provision in regard to our spouse. We are all quite eager to recognize how our wife keeps us on the straight and narrow or is our better half. We may have even acknowledged God's part in providing a spouse whose spiritual gifts fill in the gaps where our capabilities are lacking. In some cases, we may have gone as far as commenting that we are "such a great team," as our productivity as a couple seems to far exceed even the summation of our efforts.

That is all well and good. This book is about something more. It is about taking the acknowledgment of God's provision one step further. This step is a giant one because it mandates a complete change in the perspective through which a man views his wife. This perspective is founded in, and requires the full acceptance of, a single compelling assumption. I keep this assumption close to my heart. It is an assumption I cherish. It guides my daily interactions with my wife. It is the first thing I share when I counsel men with marital problems:

> *Before time began, my merciful Creator knew my every trait, good and bad—and He loved me. He foreknew my decision to place my life trust in the powerful Name and shed blood of His Son, Jesus. With His hand in my life thereby unfettered by that free-will decision of mine, God knew exactly where He wanted to take me through the course of my life. He knew He wanted to make me as much like His precious Son, Jesus, as He possibly could in the time He had allotted for me.*

With this goal for my life as His guiding priority, and with His hand freed by His foreknowledge of my trust in the name of Jesus, He desired to give me nothing less than the perfect wife. He knew she would be a very critical part of my sanctification process. He therefore considered every single woman that He would place anywhere and anytime in the entirety of His masterful creation. God left no stone unturned in His search for my perfect sanctification partner.

He knew the heart of every woman who would ever live. He knew their every answer to each one of the millions of questions He would ask throughout their lives—every single answer a free-will choice on their part. He knew how every one of them would respond to me and my traits and my decisions—both good and bad—in the daily tests He would place before me. He likewise knew how I would respond to each of these women and their traits and their decisions—both good and bad— in the daily tests He would place before them. In much less than even an instant, He knew every minute detail of every possible decision by every potential wife in every possible combination with the many free-will choices I would make in every one of the real-life circumstances He would orchestrate in my life.

And then He chose the perfect woman for me. I am married to that woman. Not only is she the perfect wife for me, but I am also God's choice as the perfect husband for her—and ours is a truly awesome God.

> *For you created my inmost being; you knit me together in my mother's womb. I praise you because I am fearfully and wonderfully made; your works are wonderful, I know that full well. My frame was not hidden from you when I was made in the secret place. When I was woven together in the depths of the earth, your eyes saw my unformed body. All the days ordained for me were written in your book before one of them came to be. How precious to me are your thoughts, O God! How vast is the sum of them!*
>
> —Psalm 139:13-17

"All the days ordained for me were written ..." What an incredible revelation. I used to view this precious scripture in such a simplistic manner. Sometimes we men tend to be concrete thinkers. I assumed it meant that God said, "Okay, you get 27,375 days." I really don't know why I took it so simply and so literally. This passage means so very much more. It means that God knows everything about us—and exactly what it will take to get us where He wants us to go. With this knowledge in hand, He planned every second of the course of our lives—all within the framework of our God-given right to choose our own response to the questions He would pose in every one of our pre-ordained days.

With this recognition of God's active hand in our every moment, the obvious next question involves the nature of the motivating purpose that guides God's hand in the planning of our lives.

Copyright 2005 Michael K. Pasque

> *And we know that in all things God works for the good of those who love him, who have been called according to his purpose. For those God foreknew he also predestined to be conformed to the likeness of his Son, that he might be the firstborn among many brothers. And those he predestined, he also called; those he called, he also justified; those he justified, he also glorified. What, then, shall we say in response to this? If God is for us, who can be against us? He who did not spare his own Son, but gave him up for us all—how will he not also, along with him, graciously give us all things?*
>
> —Romans 8:28-32 (emphasis added)

Did you ever wonder what the Holy Spirit was saying when He told us: *"For those God foreknew he also predestined to be conformed to the likeness of his Son...?"* Did you ever wonder how that applied to our lives? It is one of the most important passages in the Bible. It means that God *"foreknew"* our decision to accept the redemption offered by the shed blood of His Son, Jesus. That knowledge alone is what looses His hand in the lives of His saints—for He will not violate our freedom to accept or refuse the free gift of salvation. But, with that foreknowledge of our acceptance in hand, before time began, before He created the earth, He planned out the incredible promise found above in Romans 8:28-32. Since He foreknew our response to this, the most important question of our entire life, He then predestined the course of our life to conform us *"to the likeness of His Son"*.

> *O LORD, you have searched me and you know me. You know when I sit and when I rise; you perceive my thoughts from afar. You discern my going out and my lying down; you are familiar with all my ways. Before a word is on my tongue you know it completely, O LORD. You hem me in—behind and before; you have laid your hand upon me. Such knowledge is too wonderful for me, too lofty for me to attain. Where can I go from your Spirit? Where can I flee from your presence? If I go up to the heavens, you are there; if I make my bed in the depths, you are there. If I rise on the wings of the dawn, if I settle on the far side of the sea, even there your hand will guide me, your right hand will hold me fast.*
>
> —Psalm 139:1-10 (emphasis added)

Most certainly, the choice of our wife is an absolutely fundamental, critical part of the fulfillment of this promise of sanctification. We can be assured that she will play a critical part in the process by which God's *"hand will guide"* us and His *"right hand will hold [us] fast."* She is the most important human being we will interact with in our entire life. Our interactions with her are too important to our sanctification for God to leave the choice of our spouse up to us. Knowing that we would choose Him, God chose her to help in the process of our sanctification.

Let there be no doubt in our mind about the thoroughness with which God pursues this predestination promise of our conformance to the likeness of Jesus. This transformation is critical since we in fact have no ability whatsoever to achieve our creation purpose and our deepest heart's desire (to obey, serve, love, praise, and glorify the Father) except and only as we resemble His Son. God could not be more serious about this process. In fact, precisely this predestination—that we will become like Jesus—is the bottom-line premise behind our creation. It is the foundation. Our wife was chosen exactly for us as a critical component of this sanctification process. She is the foundation of one of the prime mechanisms by which God is going to get us where He wants us to go. It is critical that we recognize this so that we can formulate our responses, thoughts, and actions toward this woman in the correct perspective—an *eternal* frame of heart and mind.

Personally, when I view my wife as my *God-chosen* perfect spouse, it changes everything for me—as it should for you. For you also—if you are married now and have accepted the redemption offered by Jesus—are married to the perfect woman for you. The all-knowing God chose her from all of the women of the world just for you, and you alone. She is no one else's perfect wife and there is no more perfect wife for you. No matter how bad things may seem at times, no matter how low your relationship may have gotten, *if you are a follower of Christ and married to her, then she is your one and only perfect wife*.

Each and every one of the billions of other women who would live anywhere on earth for all time were considered specifically for God's plans for you—and found *wanting*. Only this woman was found to be perfect for you. Only she can get you exactly where God wants you to go.

All others were found wanting.

The importance of our acceptance of the very real truth of this basic assumption cannot be overstated. Just as the foundation of all truth in our life is found in God's Holy Word, so is the scriptural foundation for this belief found in the book of Genesis. There, we are specifically told that God chose Rebekah to be Isaac's wife.

> *See, I am standing beside this spring; if a maiden comes out to draw water and I say to her, "Please let me drink a little water from your jar," and if she says to me, "Drink, and I'll draw water for your camels too," let her be the one* the LORD has chosen *for my master's son.*

Copyright 2005 Michael K. Pasque

> *"Before I finished praying in my heart, Rebekah came out, with her jar on her shoulder."*
>
> —Genesis 24:43-45 (emphasis added)

Why is it that we are so willing to accept the fact that God chose Rebekah for Isaac, but so unwilling to see that we are no less loved by God than Isaac? God has done the same for us! Is our sanctification any less important than Isaac's? Is our wife any less important to our sanctification process than Rebekah was to Isaac's? The Holy Spirit is telling us that the choice of the single most important individual in our lives—a most intimate and critical component of the process that will turn us into the likeness of Jesus—is far too important to be left up to our wisdom, or worse yet, up to random chance. God chose Rebekah from among all of the women who would ever live precisely and specifically for His precious Isaac—and He chose our wives for us, too.

I am sure that you have read (and heard quoted at nearly every wedding ceremony you have ever attended) the words of Jesus Christ regarding divorce.

> *"Haven't you read," he replied, "that at the beginning the Creator 'made them male and female,' and said, 'For this reason a man will leave his father and mother and be united to his wife, and the two will become one flesh'? So they are no longer two, but one. Therefore <u>what God has joined together</u>, let man not separate."*
>
> —Matthew 19:4-6 (emphasis added)

I don't know about you, but when I hear the words *"what God has joined together,"* my first thought is that they refer only to the marriage ceremony itself. After all, the basis for most marriage ceremonies is a solemn oath before God. One might logically reason God gives His blessing, certification, or sanctification of the marriage between two people based upon the sacred vows that they make to each other. No doubt God's blessing and sanctification of their marriage occurs when they stand before Him and declare their unending devotion to each other for "as long as they both shall live."

Even so, let's not miss the subtle—but really not so subtle—truth underlying this foundational statement by Jesus. He is also stating that God has *actively "joined"* these two together. God planned their marriage before time began. The reference above is not just to God's passive sanctification of a random occurrence where a man and a woman just happened to find each other and decided to get married. In our simplistic, limited view of God and His interest in our daily activities, most of us actually think that *we* were responsible for choosing our

Copyright 2005 Michael K. Pasque

mates. We mistakenly think that God just said, "Oh well, I guess this marriage will be okay. Sure … I guess I can sanctify this marriage."

How it must make God wince when we so readily believe that He has so little interest in such an important part of our life. How naïve we are to think so superficially of the infinite nature of the mind of God. The deep truth behind the belief that God chose our wife for us becomes remarkably clear when we place it in the context of the omnipotent, infinitely wise God whose hand controls every atom of His magnificent creation. Jesus, in fact, is telling us that the very reason it is not okay to get divorced is because He—Almighty God—*planned this marriage from the beginning of time:*

> *" … what God has joined together, let man not separate."*
> —Matthew 19:4-6

Not only that, but if we can just trust in the infinite purity of the goodness of God, we can know in no uncertain terms that He planned the merger with our very best eternal interests in mind.

> *And we know that in all things God works for the good of those who love him, who have been called according to his purpose.*
> —Romans 8:28

The knowledge that God chose our wives for us with our very best eternal interest in mind truly does change everything, doesn't it? The implications of our deep heart belief in this fact reach far into the intricacies of our daily lives. No longer do we have to worry about what life would have been like if we had just met Cindy Crawford or Meg Ryan or Julia Roberts before we met our wife. No longer can we entertain the thought that we may have married the wrong woman. If we are married, we can be assured that our wife is exactly the one we need to get us where Almighty God wants us to go. This is God's promise to each of us. She truly is our perfect mate.

This applies even if we married our current spouse before we gave our heart to Jesus. It also applies if we have not yet given our heart to Jesus but will in the future. It even applies if our wife is not a *believer*.

> *To the rest I say this (I, not the Lord): If any brother has a wife who is not a believer and she is willing to live with him, he must not divorce her.*
> —1 Corinthians 7:12

Copyright 2005 Michael K. Pasque

God has a plan. Not one of us is outside of His plan. His hand was loosed in our life to fully implement that plan by His foreknowledge of our acceptance of the salvation offered by belief in the most holy Name of His Son Jesus. God has made a single unique choice of one very special woman for each of us. Don't be deceived. The fact that we didn't pray for the right spouse, didn't know the Lord when we met, or weren't reading the Bible when we got married doesn't negate this promise. Just because we only turned to the Lord later in our marriage doesn't mean it is okay to shed an unbelieving wife. It is not okay because God specifically planned all of these things to occur precisely the way they have occurred.

How do you know, wife, whether you will save your husband? Or, how do you know, husband, whether you will save your wife? Nevertheless, each one should retain the place in life that the Lord assigned to him and to which God has called him. This is the rule I lay down in all the churches.
—1Corinthians 7:16-17

Does the fact that your wife was not chosen in a *godly* manner change God's intense interest in your sanctification? No chance. Does the fact that your wife is not a *believer* change God's desire that you be made into the likeness of His Son, Jesus? No chance. None of this has caught God off guard. He knew it all before time began. He planned it all before time began. If you are married, your wife is your one and only God-chosen spouse.

So no longer can any of us sit and fantasize "how much better things might have been if…" No chance. God has us precisely where He wants us. He has us married to exactly the right woman. He is in charge and His planning is perfect. We need to grab any thoughts to the contrary—any thoughts that stand opposed to the knowledge of our perfectly faithful God—and throw them right out of our minds.

We can expect much opposition here. Satan and the world want us to believe that we ended up with our respective spouses only by a combination of random chance, luck, hormones, and animal desires. This perspective renders our minds and hearts fertile ground for Satan's lies. I refuse to believe it is all just random, or that luck had anything to do with it. God is so much bigger than that. He is not just sitting idly back, with half-hearted disinterest, watching what is happening. He has assured us of this in His holy Word. For it really is not about you and me. It is about Him, and Him alone. It is all about *His* will in our life, not ours.

Your wife is a very special woman. God created her with unique and wonderful qualities. Those unique qualities of hers, even the irritating ones, are in fact perfect for you—just like my wife's traits are perfect for me. They are never a reason for a fight. They are never a reason for us to raise our needs above those of our wife. They are never an excuse to harbor ill feelings toward her. And they are never a justification to grumble before God.

It is exactly for this reason that when I am asked about my wife or my marriage I often answer, "I am married to the greatest woman in the whole world!" I am sure that statement is most often taken as hyperbole. The fact remains, however, that taken in the context of the eternal perspective of the Mighty God, for me and for you—*it is true.*

Chapter 2

The Fallout That Results From Truly Believing This

<u>Assumption # 2</u>
She is your wife until death.

    The assumption that Almighty God put this exact woman in the middle of our every day to fulfill His plan for our life is awesome in many respects. First of all, this assumption leaves no room for questions about *dumping* her.
    Don't act like you've never thought about that.
    I know you have, because that is one of Satan's favorite ploys. He wants us to sit and stew about the possibility of just eliminating our marital problems by simply unloading our wife. He wants us to sit and crave our lost freedom. He wants us to dwell on what it would be like without the headaches that come along with being married *to her*. He always hits us with these thoughts when we are tired, when our guard is down, and right in the middle of a marital disagreement.
    God, and God alone, is responsible for our meeting and marrying the woman we call our wife. Leaving her is not an option—period. This is simply not negotiable. She is our wife, our *only* wife, and she is our wife because God said so—no matter how much we think we had to do with it.
    So, we *will* live with this woman for the rest of our life. We *will* love this woman for the rest of our life. We *will* serve this woman for the rest of our life. All of this is by the decree of no one less than Almighty God.
    Our responsibility to persevere in obedience to God's will in our marital relationship is clear. This responsibility starts with the guarding of our hearts and the close attention to the messages that we allow to enter this most vulnerable heart of ours. We will not listen to Satan. When he casts negative thoughts into our mind we will not dwell on leaving our wife, even as a remote possibility. We will not crave lost freedom. We will not let our minds wander and dream of that other *perfect* woman. We will not plot and scheme and manipulate. We will not dwell on thoughts of old girlfriends or favorite movie stars. When Satan throws such thoughts into our mind, we will grab them and cast them immediately to the foot of the cross where that battle has already been fought and won for us. For that perfect

woman we desire is, in fact, the exact one God has already given us to be our wife for the rest of our life. We may be blind to this fact sometimes, but our blindness does not make it any less true.

When we start from this wonderful assumption, it makes life a lot easier. We don't have to sit and wonder if she is the right one. We are married to her so, by definition, she is the right one. We must not buy into the bill of goods Satan is trying to sell us that maybe we missed the one God *really* had planned for us. That is nonsense sent straight from the depths of hell. The acceptance of this assumption, that she is the one and only one for us, totally eliminates a million problems that modern man is challenged with by the so-called wisdom of the world. Life actually gets easier doing things God's way!

I can give you a very specific example of one way that life gets easier—*the husband trap*. You know what I'm talking about—the old *lose-lose* scenarios that women seem to be so good at constructing for their husbands. Let me give you an example from my life that occurred just last week. My wife and I were watching a Tom Hanks/Meg Ryan movie. She thinks Meg Ryan is a cutie. I do, too. So, in the middle of the movie, after a really endearing Meg Ryan scene, my wife leans over—here comes the trap—and in a joking (but you know it's not really joking) manner says, "You'd leave me for Meg Ryan, wouldn't you?"

This is one of my wife's favorite routines. You know as well as I know that I can tell her it just isn't true until I'm blue in the face. Yet she is still going to say, in great disbelief, "Oh, sure!" There is no right answer—thus the designation as a *lose-lose* husband trap.

So, by God's unending grace—and before she got another word out of her mouth—I leaned toward her, looked deep into her eyes, and whispered, "Before time began, Meg Ryan was evaluated by Almighty God as a possible wife for me. She was found *wanting*."

"Wanting?"

"Wanting."

For as long as I live, I will never forget the flicker of a smile and the look of complete wonderment on my wife's face. Her eyes looked directly into mine, and right through them into the very heart of God. She was speechless. In that moment she knew a peace and a joy that can only be known in the promise that is our loving God. He reassured her like I could never, even if I had spoken a million emphatic words.

And it was a very good day indeed.

Copyright 2005 Michael K. Pasque

Chapter 3

The List

Assumption # 3
Everything about her was chosen exactly for you.

If we truly believe that God chose our wife specifically for us, this belief should result in a change in our perspective and thus a change in our thoughts and actions toward her. A true change in perspective should always result in a change in the way we assess and respond to each new situation. How? Let's start with the most obvious. Let's talk about those little things our wife does that drive us up the wall—and our response to them. More specifically, let's consider the answer to this one revealing question: Do you have a little mental list of things she does that you secretly pray about, that you ask the Lord to change?

I know I did.

You know what I'm referring to—those things our wife does that really annoy us. We may have first recognized them when we were courting. They were a mild annoyance then and we let them slip. They were easily overlooked because we had finally found, very possibly, the most perfect woman in the whole world. After all, they were little things and we just knew that *love would conquer all.*

But now, on occasion, these annoyances really get to us. We initially tried to gently correct them. Sometimes a lively *discussion* ensued during which we again, maybe not so gently this time, tried to correct them. But, the response that our little corrective comments may have generated was a bit more of a *push back* than we care to endure again—so, now we pray about them. When conflicts arise over these issues, we quietly go to the Lord and ask Him to correct our wife's problems. *Lord, when are You going to address these problems with my wife? How much longer will I have to endure these problems of hers?*

Let's start this discussion by giving ourselves some credit here. After all, at least we are not making these problems a trigger point for heated "discussions" anymore. That is a good first step. At least we are entrusting them to the Lord instead of trying to force the kind of change upon our spouse that most assuredly would trigger more conflict. So, we're off to a pretty good start.

But you and I both know that God wants more than this from us. Stopping the conflict over these little problems is clearly the first step. But perhaps it's time to expand our response a bit further. Perhaps it's time to consider exactly where God is trying to take us with these little problems. After all, we may have been praying for quite some time for the Lord to change her, with little evidence suggesting significant progress. I know this was true in my case. Obviously we have a problem here. The problem is that God will not go against His will in answering our prayers. God wasn't answering my prayer for change in my wife because that was in fact not the change He desired.

Indeed, the Lord really does have a different change in mind. He really does want us to take this issue of conflict resolution just a step further. That step might be in a different direction than most of us would think. After all, when we strip away all of the emotional trappings the world attaches to this common setting of marital conflict, one thing becomes readily apparent. This really is not about changing our wife. It most certainly is not about changing her relationship with the Lord—it is about changing *ours*.

So, let's look at this whole scenario with a fresh perspective, a Biblically based perspective. The Word of God, in point of fact, is quite clear in this matter. It would suggest that we should be looking inside *our* hearts instead of sticking our nose into our wife's relationship with God.

> *How can you say to your brother, "Let me take the speck out of your eye," when all the time there is a plank in your own eye?*
> —Matthew 7:4

Could it be possible that God wants *us* to humble ourselves before Him in regard to these exact areas of our wife's behavior so He can reveal the parts of our own heart that we have not surrendered to Him? After all, these are the precise hidden areas of our heart that are responsible for reflexively generating our emotional, non-servant, and self-serving responses to our wife's bothersome activities. These responses are the exact ones that so often trigger or perpetuate the arguments between us.

God is trying to tell us something here. We need to completely change our point of view regarding our wife's troublesome personality traits. We need to begin to look upon those traits that we so readily condemn in our wife as God's invitation for us to know our own heart better and, therefore, for us to know Him better. They are in fact the key to the most difficult part of our sanctification process.

More precisely, these traits that cause us such dismay are not just an invitation to know Jesus better, but are also an exact roadmap to getting there. You guessed it. I am proposing that the exact *bad* traits that have us so bent out of shape are precisely the foils against which God wants us to spar. The foundational hypothesis must therefore be that there is a deep-seated reason why those particular traits of hers bother us so much—and God wants to uncover that reason, that imperfection in our hearts, so He can deal with it.

> *Search me, O God, and know my heart; test me and know my anxious thoughts. See if there is any offensive way in me, and lead me in the way everlasting.*
> —Psalm 139:23-24

The cleansing of these hidden areas of our heart, God's temple, is clearly a pivotal and everlasting part of our sanctification.

Those peculiar emotional responses of ours that we have linked to her annoying habits are specific to *our* heart. This becomes especially apparent when we realize that often other people can interact closely with our wife without any problems in these particular areas. Hard to believe? Let me ask you a question. Have you ever tried to tell a friend, an accountability partner, or even a marital counselor about one of your wife's peculiarities, only to have them look at you with a blank stare? You've got it—they don't know what we're talking about. They simply don't see it. They don't see it precisely because she is *our* perfect mate, not theirs. Indeed, she is the very chalkboard upon which God has written our very unique homework assignment. School is in session and graduation day will only arrive when we stand before the Father reflecting the image of His Son.

> *And we, who with unveiled faces all reflect the Lord's glory, are being transformed into his likeness with ever-increasing glory, which comes from the Lord, who is the Spirit.*
> —2Corinthians 3:18

> *So it is written: "The first man Adam became a living being"; the last Adam, a life-giving spirit. The spiritual did not come first, but the natural, and after that the spiritual. The first man was of the dust of the earth, the second man from heaven. As was the earthly man, so are those who are of the earth; and as is the man from heaven, so also are those who are of heaven. And just as we have borne the likeness of the earthly man, so shall we bear the likeness of the man from heaven.*
> —1Corinthians 15:45-49

God knows exactly what parts of our heart He wants to change. More often than not, however, we don't. This is especially true regarding the deep-heart, hidden issues of pride. So how does He bring the change about? He must confront us with the exact, divinely placed instrument in our lives that will trigger the introspection in our hearts that He knows we so desperately need.

Why is all of this necessary? Primarily because those attributes that God wishes to change are so totally hidden from us that they remain unrecognized by our day-to-day routine introspection. This is hidden sin. Sin hidden by the blindness that always accompanies sin. We can't change our sinful attitudes and behaviors because we are so blind toward them we don't even recognize them as sin. This is precisely why those attributes of our wife are so necessary to our sanctification process. They are the roadmap. They are critical to removing the blinders from our eyes that conceal our hidden sin—so that God can help us deal with it.

Have you ever asked God to show you your hidden sin? David did. He told us all about it in Psalm 19:

> *The law of the LORD is perfect, reviving the soul. The statutes of the LORD are trustworthy, making wise the simple. The precepts of the LORD are right, giving joy to the heart. The commands of the LORD are radiant, giving light to the eyes. The fear of the LORD is pure, enduring forever. The ordinances of the LORD are sure and altogether righteous. They are more precious than gold, than much pure gold; they are sweeter than honey, than honey from the comb. By them is your servant warned; in keeping them there is great reward. <u>Who can discern his errors? Forgive my hidden faults.</u>*
>
> *Keep your servant also from willful sins; may they not rule over me. Then will I be blameless, innocent of great transgression. May the words of my mouth and the meditation of my heart be pleasing in your sight, O LORD, my Rock and my Redeemer.*
>
> —Psalm 19:7-14 (emphasis added)

Truly, our hidden sin resembles the many layers of an onion. As we peel each layer of sin off, another appears that we did not even know existed.

Indeed, our wife—and all the other people God sends into our life—are messengers bearing news from God. The only way He can get us to grow is to first make us aware of our sin. Only then can He help us work through the needed changes in our thoughts and behavior. But the first step of discernment is the key, and discernment is exactly what our wife's attitude and behavior "problems" are all about. Not only do we need to know what our sin is, but we need to understand the feelings generated in our heart that cause us to go down these dark pathways. We need to fully expose the self-righteous feelings our rebellious spirit generates in this regard—and our wife is the searchlight. She is nothing less than God's messenger in our life. She is the chalkboard. She is the foil. She is our sacred revealer from God.

And that is why our relationship with our wife is so precious to the Lord. He knew that only a very special, incredibly intimate relationship with another person—*a wife* to be exact—could be the vehicle required to get to the real nitty-gritty stuff in the deepest reaches of our heart. He wants it all cleaned up in the process of our sanctification, the process of turning us into the very rich and precious likeness of His Son, Jesus.

Chapter 4

Getting At the Deep Heart Issues

Assumption # 4
Pride is the taproot sin that ensnares your marriage.

We have established the foundational premise that the intimate nature of the God-ordained marriage relationship is the primary setting in which the Holy Spirit can tackle the really tough issues in our individual sanctification. These really deep-rooted issues almost always have to do with the taproot sin of *pride*. Pride is so deeply ingrained in our hearts that without Jesus we, for all intents and purposes, are powerless over its hold on us. Left to our own devices, there really is no hope of even recognizing the heart-deep pride issues, let alone changing them.

Once our prideful heart issues are fully recognized and their hold over us acknowledged, however, they can then be given over to the sanctifying power of Jesus Christ. There is no other power that can defeat the entrenched, dominating authority that pride has over our human nature.

> *For Christ did not send me to baptize, but to preach the gospel—not with words of human wisdom, lest the cross of Christ be emptied of <u>its power</u>. For the message of the cross is foolishness to those who are perishing, but to us who are being saved it is <u>the power of God</u>.*
> —1Corinthians 1:17-18 (emphasis added)

In dealing with pride in our marital relationship, the power of the cross of Christ is our only hope. The crucifixion of Jesus was awesomely and precisely about our salvation, but it was not exclusively about salvation. It was also most magnificently about sanctification. Just as we are powerless to redeem ourselves, we are also powerless to complete the incredible process of our sanctification. Jesus does both tasks for us.

> *Let us fix our eyes on Jesus, <u>the author and perfecter of our faith</u>, who for the joy set before him endured the cross, scorning its shame, and sat down at the right hand of the throne of God.*
> —Hebrews 12:2 (emphasis added)

Copyright 2005 Michael K. Pasque

It is only through the power of Jesus Christ, as demonstrated in His victory on the cross, that we are able to undergo the deep transformation process—the defeat of the intense pride of our heart—that is necessary to change our human frailty into the character of Jesus.

God knows that we can't defeat these deep-rooted sins of our heart if we can't even recognize them. Indeed, our wife's specific ability to reveal that which no one else can reveal—often the issues that no one else even knows about—should be further confirmation to each of us that our marriage was no random event. Her distinct character traits were not just placed in our life by happenstance. We know this because we know there is nothing random about our sanctification process. It is most specifically and most preciously about the Person of Jesus Christ. God would never leave something that important up to us. God's mastery is seen in every step of our sanctification process because He is in complete control of it. The way that our wife's peculiar traits bother us is not only not random, it is *precise*. These traits of hers are trigger points that set off reflexive defensive maneuvers that are rooted deep in our hearts. They engender this type of heightened response for a reason. We strike out most violently against the things that strike closest to our hearts. These specially God-chosen traits of hers are no different.

This Christ-oriented perspective toward the personality traits of our God-ordained spouse must necessarily challenge each one of us: we must take that list we talked about in the last chapter and begin to pray and meditate about each and every one of our wife's bothersome traits. We must dwell in the throne room of God as we humble our heart in regard to these problems. Then, when we have uncovered the deep heart sins that our interactions with our wife have led us to, it is critical that we respond to them and to the feelings behind them in a manner that pleases God. The nature of our response is our choice. We can always do what I have done for nearly all of my life and respond from a prideful heart. This prideful heart of mine is the source of such endearing thoughts as, "This is her problem" or "What is wrong with her" or "How I wish God would change her heart." No progress is made in my sanctification, in my relationships with Jesus and with my wife, when I respond this way.

If, however, I go to God with a meek heart and humbly admit my weakness, a different response occurs. In this humbled state, I can no longer gloss over sin and blame everything on my wife. I know what I am talking about here. I was the king of pride in my relationship with my magnificent wife. It was *always* her fault. It was always *her* problem. It was always her that God needed to chasten, not me. But, as God has peeled back the covering of my sin and revealed the true nature of my heart, I have humbly realized that in every single one of "my wife's problem

Copyright 2005 Michael K. Pasque

areas," *I was the one who was at fault*. I am not just being modest here. I have come to realize that these areas in which I was critical of my wife were in fact the precise areas of *my* weakness! The whole mess that resulted, including her sometimes less than optimal responses, was my fault, not hers.

Let me give you a simple example of how my relationship with my wife is helping to gradually unravel the web of pride that ensnares my heart. Although this is no earth-shaking example, it is quite informative and I am sure quite common. It is, in fact, precisely in little incidents like these that the real work gets done. This is where God really begins changing our hearts.

I used to continually struggle against my wife during my weekends off. I'm as busy as I can be during the week and also find myself working hard on at least one or two weekends a month. As a result, I used to be pretty choosy about what I did on my weekends off. As you might guess, my well-made weekend plans did not always align with my wife's desires. My *manly* project list was simply not the same as her *honey-do* list.

The conflict continued with occasional escalation until the Holy Spirit finally led my stubborn heart to some serious introspection about the problem. Through His guidance alone, I realized that my priorities were simply wrong and that my faithful Savior was trying to enrich my understanding of the misalignment that had obviously occurred. But, the realignment of my priorities was just the tip of the iceberg. Through God's never-ending grace, my eyes were opened to the deeper problem: the pride-filled, selfish, non-servant attitude toward my wife that characterized my daily interactions with her. Marriage is about submitting. My job is to serve her and her interests. Instead, I was continually and persistently raising my interests and my priorities above those of my wife. I was clearly treating my priorities as significant and hers as trivial.

I initially did not have a clue what kind of message I was sending to my life-partner. But our actions always reveal the true attitude of our hearts and spouses seem to be particularly adept at telling when their welfare is not a priority to us. They sense a lack of concern. My wife is good at this. But she really didn't have to be, since my offense against her was so blatant. We can say, "I love you" until we are blue in the face. But if our actions and attitudes clearly demonstrate a lack of concern for the things that burden our wife, we're wasting our breath.

Now, I plan my weekends totally around my wife. She is my first weekend priority. I start every weekend by asking her what her plans are. Even if she can't come up with any projects, I look around for things that I know are important to her and make them my main concerns for the weekend. I try to take the kids everywhere they need to be, fix all the things on her *honey-do* list, take her out to dinner, and wash the dishes when we eat at home, to name just a few.

Copyright 2005 Michael K. Pasque

The world and the Lord of the Flies continually try to tell me this just isn't right: "What are you thinking? You've earned this weekend off! Don't you get to have any fun in your life? If she really loved you, she would cut you a little slack on the weekends." Sound familiar? It should. These are Satan's weekend lies. They are whispered into the hearts of men everywhere. They have a common thread running through all of them. They each rationalize the raising of our priorities above those of our wife. These lies are worldly wisdom in its purest form. They fly in the face of our faith in, our knowledge of, and our trust in our God and Redeemer. They fly in the face of His holy Word. By their very definition, they accept as fact one of Satan's greatest deceptions—that what God wants for our life just has to be a whole lot less fun than what the world has planned for us. What a lie! All God wants us to do is to trust Him in this regard. He is ready to take our blinders off and truly set us free in His will. Indeed, we are truly free only when we are dead center in the middle of His, not our will for our lives—and His will is that we model the humble servanthood of Jesus in our interaction with our wife.

> *Husbands, love your wives, just as Christ loved the church and gave himself up for her to make her holy, cleansing her by the washing with water through the word, and to present her to himself as a radiant church, without stain or wrinkle or any other blemish, but holy and blameless.*
>
> —Ephesians 5:25-26

God's will in our lives is made clear in His holy Word. His Word is truth. Humble servanthood toward our wife is truth. Placing her interests above ours is truth. And, as usual, the truth in this case (and in all cases) is found in the exact opposite direction of the rhetoric, logic, wisdom, and intelligence of the world.

> *The Lord says: "These people come near to me with their mouth and honor me with their lips, but their hearts are far from me. Their worship of me is made up only of rules taught by men. Therefore once more I will astound these people with wonder upon wonder; the wisdom of the wise will perish, the intelligence of the intelligent will vanish."*
>
> —Isaiah 29:13-14

I know what you're thinking. You're thinking, "What about *my* life? How can I make her my every priority? Where will it all end? If I give her an inch, she will take a mile. I will be left with nothing. How can I place such a priority on her alone?"

Copyright 2005 Michael K. Pasque

I had the same thoughts initially when the Holy Spirit brought me to this point in my relationship with my wife. That was before I acknowledged that, contrary to what the world would have us believe, this is precisely what life as a believer is all about. Life with Jesus is all about loving, honoring, and serving the people He brings into our lives every single day. This isn't some sidebar. It isn't some casual observance that we take care of after we have dealt with *our* priorities. It isn't activity reserved only for super Christians. This is the whole show! Further still, of all the people God brings into my life every day—every one of them a test of my willingness to obey—my wife is the most important. She is the one I will know most intimately in all of my life. She isn't some minor priority in my life. She is the star of the main show and loving her is absolutely critical in my walk with Jesus.

So, I *do* need to make her my priority. I *do* need to make her my whole weekend. I *do* need to go out of my way to serve her.

How God has blessed this commitment! When I make my wife my priority, He gives me all sorts of fun times and even frees up more weekend time for things I want to do than I ever could have "arranged" on my own. He is such a faithful God. I thoroughly enjoy my weekends now. I have come to enjoy things on my wife's list of priorities that I never thought I would have any chance of enjoying. Now when I finish my weekends, I look back on them and feel great! No longer is there the empty feeling that always follows a weekend characterized only by the futility of trying to make myself happy. God is so perfectly faithful. And once again, I was the one who had things wrong, not my wife.

I don't know about you, but I can use all of the help I can get in this venture. And true to God's promise, the Holy Spirit is always there to remind me when I wander off this path of marital servanthood. I can always tell when I am no longer humbling myself before my wife and her desires and priorities. That is always when the tensions mount and everyone gets a little edgy. And always—always—I am the one who can fix it. I can fix it single-handedly. All I have to do is humble myself and the healing power of Almighty God flows down upon my home like a refreshing spring rain. When I realize I haven't been humbling myself, what a delight it is to run to my wife to apologize and seek her forgiveness. For in humbling ourselves is found the true measure of our integrity in Christ—and does it ever feel good!

The fact that this feels so good should not come as a surprise to us. It feels good because this whole thing is about Him, not about us. We are wired to seek Him and please Him and it is a very special feeling indeed when we seek God by humbling ourselves. I practically run to do it when the Holy Spirit wakes me up out of my self-focused stupor. I run to do it because I know it is my precious Savior's will in my life. I run to do it because it honors Him. I run to do it because

Copyright 2005 Michael K. Pasque

I fear God. I run to do it because humbling oneself is activity that is, in my life, uniformly rewarded by God. I run to do it because by humbling myself before God by humbling myself before my wife, I unleash the *"incomparably great power"* of God in my life and in my marriage.

> *I pray also that the eyes of your heart may be enlightened in order that you may know the hope to which he has called you, the riches of his glorious inheritance in the saints, and his incomparably great power for us who believe. That power is like the working of his mighty strength, which he exerted in Christ when he raised him from the dead and seated him at his right hand in the heavenly realms, far above all rule and authority, power and dominion, and every title that can be given, not only in the present age but also in the one to come. And God placed all things under his feet and appointed him to be head over everything for the church, which is his body, the fullness of him who fills everything in every way.*
>
> —Ephesians 1:18-23

I also run to humble myself before my wife because I know that when I do, I will get to see God go to work right in front of me. He will melt my wife's heart. He really will—right there in front of me. He does it all the time. I get to witness God at work in my life right before my very eyes. Now *that* is true freedom, freedom to choose to obey. Freedom to know the only touch that really satisfies as I feel Jesus brush by me in these close combat encounters. I run to this because it is wonderful. In every respect, it is wonderful. It is the pure joy of the knowledge of the Living God. It resonates like a chord played on the most secret heartstrings of my very soul. What a God, indeed.

Still not convinced you want to venture out on that precarious humility ledge on a daily basis? Let me ask you another question. Do you, as a reader of the Word of God, think there is any remote chance that God would punish you, refuse to rescue you, make fun of you in front of the angels, hold it against you in any way, or just think you are really stupid because you, in His Name, chose to humble yourself before your wife? No chance.

No chance.

So, I challenge you to go ahead and make that list that we discussed in the last chapter. Write down all of those things your wife does that really bother you. This time, however, we are going to put a different title at the top of the page. It should read in big bold letters something like:

Chances to Know and Move Closer to God!

Copyright 2005 Michael K. Pasque

Then, go to work on your list. I'm already working on mine. It takes time, meditation, and prayer. It takes hard work. But it is an absolutely critical list that we will be working on for the rest of our life. In the meanwhile, we can keep that piece of paper tucked away in a secret place and pull it out from time to time to marvel at how our faithful Savior is completing His good work in us. For our wife was chosen for us precisely because of those unique traits of hers. They aren't just to aggravate us. They are there to get our attention. They are there to shine a light, God's revealing light, into the deep recesses of our heart. They are there to direct our path through the tough part of our sanctification. They are there to make us into a man of God—a man who seeks to defeat the pride of his heart and humble himself before the will of his Savior.

Copyright 2005 Michael K. Pasque

Chapter 5

"Love Each Other"—the Command To Love

Assumption # 5
Your interaction with your wife is the very focal point, in your entire life, of God's specific command to you to "love each other."

If you are a guy like me—which you are—you have an innate, God given, deep-rooted desire to cut through all of the garbage in this life and get to the *bottom-line*. That bottom-line is centered on the most important issue in our lives. It is the very reason for our existence. It is the answer to the question, "What is life all about?"

The answer to this question is easily known if you have given your heart to the King of kings. I am going to assume that you have. I am going to assume that Jesus is the Lord of your life and your heart's cry is to know and love and glorify God. For Christians, that is the bottom-line. The foremost problem for many of us, however, is in knowing what this means in the context of our everyday lives. How exactly do we know, love, and glorify God on a day-to-day basis?

This dilemma is the very mettle of life itself—and the answer to the dilemma is found only in the Word of God. In fact, this dilemma is the reason the Bible is written the way it is. It tells stories about the working of God in the everyday lives of many, widely differing men and women. As such, it is *the* guide to applying God's specific directions to know, love and glorify Him in the setting of our daily life situations.

So the key principles of the Bible become *"a lamp to my feet and a light to my path"* (Psalm 119:105) when it comes to making the many decisions that must be made in the course of any given day. This is why daily reading of the Word of God is so critical. This daily reading is the only way to engrave God's fundamental commands so deeply on our hearts and in our minds that they are our automatic response when we are suddenly confronted by God's testing.

Copyright 2005 Michael K. Pasque

For out of the overflow of the heart the mouth speaks.
—Matthew 12:34-37

What exactly are these *key principles*, these fundamental commands? There are many different ways the Holy Spirit has chosen to emphasize key principles in the Word of God. The most obvious is simple repetition. Pivotal scriptures are repeated over and over again. This is where we get to the point of this chapter and the subject of this book. Did you know that the commands to *"love each other," "love one another," "love your neighbor,"* or *"love your enemies"* are repeated no less than 26 times in the New Testament? Not just 5 times or 10 times—which would be remarkable in itself. 26 times. Do you think that someone was trying to make a point?

Indeed, the Gospel accounts themselves leave no question of how Jesus felt about these words. He laid singular emphasis on this command to love in a very special set of passages from the Gospel of John. He introduced the command to love by tying a key statement to it. Right up front He makes the critical connection between loving Him and *obeying* Him. Do you want to know how to get right to the bottom-line? *Do you want to know how to love God?* Jesus tells us exactly how, in no uncertain terms.

If you love me, you will obey what I command.
—John 14:15

Jesus Himself has directly told us, in clear-cut, straightforward language, that if we truly love our Savior *then we will obey what He commands*. John spells it out even more specifically when he states:

This is love for God: to obey his commands.
—1John 5:3 (emphasis added)

Do you really want to love Jesus? We all say that it is the cry of our hearts—and no doubt it is. But, have you figured out exactly what that means? Are you sure that your interpretation of what that means and God's interpretation of what that means are the same? Do you know for sure that you love Him the way *He* wants to be loved?

The answers to those questions are the beauty and the pure joy of the above Scripture passage. It defines exactly how we are to go about loving God. Right out of the mouth of Jesus we are told, plainly and simply, that if we love Jesus, we will obey what He commands. What, exactly, does He command? Once again, it is spelled out plainly—so there can be no confusion—only a few verses later in the very same Gospel of John.

> *This is my command: Love each other.*
>
> —John 15:17

That's *"command"* in the singular, not in the plural. Not the *Ten* Commandment<u>s</u>. Not the *two* great commandment<u>s</u>. Simply the clear-cut, well-defined, singular command that follows—*"Love each other."*

As I stated above, I am a concrete-thinking, cut-and-dried kind of guy, a bottom-line seeker. I want to cut through all the other stuff and grab ferociously and tenaciously to the real message, the bottom-line. For the bottom-line is precisely what my simple mind reflexively brings to the surface when the battle intensifies. When chaos rules on my daily field of conflict, when in the frenzy of the battle, there is only time for reflex actions. This is especially true in my interactions with my wife. I need that bottom-line. I need it first and foremost in the front of my mind when I'm praying and, of perhaps more importance, I need it first and foremost in the front of my heart when I am reacting reflexively to my wife.

For it is our day-to-day reactions to the ambushes, the sudden catastrophes, the mood swings, the family challenges—all of which seem to sweep in riding a torrent of emotion—that determine the tenor of our relationship with our most precious life partner. Our reflexive reactions to these situations are governed, as Jesus clearly spelled out above, by the priorities of our heart. So, our *bottom-line* beliefs are going to rule the day. They are going to determine our actions. They are going to be our demonstration of whether we really believe in the Name of Jesus or whether we only give *His* priorities lip service in our life.

And this is it—the bottom-line—*"Love each other."* This is truly a unique statement in the Bible. It is, nonetheless, so common and familiar to us that we almost always read past it quickly and gloss over the importance that this statement should have in our life. We miss its real intent and potential impact on our relationship with the most significant *"other"* in our lives. But, let there be no doubt in your mind, it is *the* bottom-line. It is unequivocal and its words are chosen carefully, even down to the letter. The lack of an *"s"* on the end of the word *"command"* is not a typo. The Holy Spirit of the Living God is not in the habit of making typos. It is stated exactly as the Holy Spirit wanted it stated. Clearly, Jesus must have said it this way for a reason: possibly—just possibly—to drive home the point that this is *the* command. That truly loving and worshiping God—the greatest of all commandments—is all encompassed in obeying this single command to *"Love each other."*

Copyright 2005 Michael K. Pasque

So, besides the obvious, what does this have to do with our relationship with our wife? Why exactly have I spent so much time making this point? Well, based on the quotes above, the answers to these questions depend on how you define *"each other"* or *"one another."* It may even depend on how you define *"your neighbor"* or even *"your enemies."* But, if you define them such that the above passages mean that you are to love God by loving all of the people that He brings into contact with you every day, then most likely ... *your wife is the single person who most intensely embodies the focal point of the command of Jesus to "Love each other."*

No doubt the command applies to all, but most significantly it applies to our God-given spouse in a unique and special manner. She is our closest friend and, because of the very intimacy she shares with us, she can be our most empowered enemy. For most of us, there is no other person we will encounter in our lives with whom we will spend more time in rigorous, intense interaction. Loving her is the most significant and probably the most difficult test of this command that we will encounter in our lifetime.

Where am I going with all this? We all think we recognize how important our relationship with our wife is, but do we really? Perhaps in no other relationship does the reality that "familiarity breeds contempt" more aptly apply. But it is this exact familiarity that reminds us that, for the majority of us, there is *no other human being in the world* with whom we will interact more—whether judged in quantity, quality or intensity of relationship—than our wife. The conclusion is pretty clear. If we are married, then no other person who fits the Biblical description of *"each other"* in the passage from John deserves more attention than our wife. If we place any other human relationship above our relationship with her, then we are deceived. Indeed, in our whole life the single most important way that we will love God *is by loving our wife*. This raises our relationship with her to a whole new level.

Our relationship with our wife is the very focal point of our relationship with, and our love for, Jesus Christ. If we really desire to love Him—which must be the cry of every believer's heart—then genuinely loving her, selflessly, unconditionally, and in humble servanthood, is not just an option, it is the whole ball game.

Copyright 2005 Michael K. Pasque

Chapter 6

"If It Ain't Right…"

<u>Assumption #6</u>
If your relationship with your wife is not right, then don't kid yourself; your relationship with Almighty God is not right either.

If we are to believe, then, that our relationship with our wife is the single most important embodiment of our day-to-day relationship with God, then the next key assumption logically follows: *If our relationship with our wife is not right, even in the smallest of areas, anytime and all the time, then our relationship with Jesus Christ is not right either.*

Hard truth. But we all know it is truth. Too many of us nonetheless continue to act like these two critical relationships are separate and unrelated. We act like everything can be "just fine, thank you very much" in our walk with the Lord while raging warfare breaks out every evening when we get home from work. By the truth found in the Word of God, however, our premise must be that discord in our marriage and a heart truly surrendered to Jesus are diametrically opposed to, and entirely inconsistent with each other. They cannot exist together.

This moves this whole discussion of our day-to-day relationship with our wife to a completely different level. Nothing is more important to anyone who calls himself a Christian than being in the right relationship with Jesus Christ. To walk with Him like Enoch, to see His face like Moses, to visit His throne room like Isaiah, and to run hard after His heart like David are nothing less than the deepest desires of our heart. Knowing, loving, and serving Jesus is the cry of our hearts because He, in His perfect wisdom, made us precisely that way. It is in our DNA. It is the way we are constructed. It is the *fact* behind every thing that we call *self*. Knowing and glorifying Him by our obedient love is behind every good and wholesome desire we ever express in our thoughts and our deeds. The resulting intimate knowledge of Him is the only thing that satisfies. Knowing Him in the humbled love of an obedient servant is—precisely and exclusively—what life is all about.

This relationship with Jesus isn't a small part of the game. It isn't even a large part of the game. It is nothing less than the *whole* game. It isn't the secondary

Copyright 2005 Michael K. Pasque

objective of our lives. In fact, even to call it the primary objective understates reality—for it is the *only* objective. It is the first objective on a list of one. It isn't something we do in our spare time. It isn't a hobby. It doesn't just happen on Sunday mornings. It isn't something we get to when we get a chance after tending to all of life's other little issues. It is *the* issue. It is the only issue. It is all that will be left when our world melts away on that impending great and awesome *"day of the Lord"* (Isaiah 13:6). For Jesus is before and above *all* things. This is the undeniable truth that should rule over every minute of our lives.

> *Your attitude should be the same as that of Christ Jesus: Who, being in very nature God, did not consider equality with God something to be grasped, but made himself nothing, taking the very nature of a servant, being made in human likeness. And being found in appearance as a man, he humbled himself and became obedient to death—even death on a cross! Therefore God exalted him to the highest place and gave him the name that is above every name, that at the name of Jesus every knee should bow, in heaven and on earth and under the earth, and every tongue confess that Jesus Christ is Lord, to the glory of God the Father.*
>
> —Philippians 2:5-11 (emphasis added)

This truth elevates our relationship with our wife to a much higher level than even the best among us would normally ascribe to it. Our relationship with her is not about focusing on her problems, her guilt, or her fault in our marital discord. It is instead about nothing less than the Creator of the universe. Even so, I can't tell you how many times I have interacted with men who seem so self-satisfied in their walk with the Lord while all the while carrying on a near continual battle with their wives. How easy it is for all of us to act like it is all *her* problem and that everything is just fine with *our* relationship with God. How easy it is to deceive ourselves into believing that these are separate issues—that we can somehow compartmentalize them—that we can be okay with God when we are so very not okay with our wife. In this regard, I have personally reached new heights in redefining the word *self-righteous* in the way I have treated my wife.

Truly loving our wife is about truly loving Jesus. Truly loving Jesus is about truly loving our wife. Jesus is love. He is the ultimate servant. He put the Father's will first in everything. If we can't model him in our relationship with our wife, *then we do not have it right*. Period. And when we are modeling His life perfectly by meekly placing ourselves in the same position of humble servanthood that Jesus modeled, then, as a direct result, our relationship with our wife cannot help but be perfect.

Copyright 2005 Michael K. Pasque

We all need to take a long, hard look at our wife. She is our barometer. Our ongoing relationship with her serves as a gauge that can give us a highly accurate, real-time reading on the current status of the most important relationship of our life—our relationship with Jesus Christ.

.

Chapter 7

Let's Get This Straight Right Now

Assumption #7
Everything that is wrong with your marriage is, in fact, your fault.

Before we get one more step into this discussion, we have to get one thing perfectly clear. It follows directly from the discussion in the last chapter. It is a direct reflection of a heart that is truly humbled before God and wife. It is an assumption that should be obvious to the truly surrendered heart. It must be made. It must be made on your part and it must be made on my part. We must wholeheartedly and without reservation or condition accept it and its implications. It should change our perspective and therefore our behavior. It must guide every step we make toward our wives from this day forward, so we really have to believe it. That means we don't go any further with this until we believe it, understand it, and make it a part of our consciousness every second of every minute that we spend in the presence of our wives.

Do I have your attention? Okay, then.

Our assumption, from the beginning until the end, must be that all of the bad stuff that has happened in our relationship with our wife is *entirely our fault.*

From the moment that we begin to roll this assumption around in our hearts, size it up, take it for its face value and really begin to give it the credence it deserves—from that moment on we have a chance. We have a chance to salvage that which God has joined together and which we, by our sin, have torn apart.

I know what you are thinking, because I have had the same thoughts: "Wait a minute. She is not without fault in this whole thing. She has clearly overstepped some boundaries. She has clearly sinned. She is not some perfect, snowy-white, clear-conscience victim in this real life melodrama."

Agreed.

Seriously.

I concede that point.

But that doesn't have anything to do with it.

Her guilt or innocence is not what we are discussing. They have nothing in the world to do with this assumption. This assumption is about preparing our heart the way our Savior wants us to prepare it for the battle ahead. This assumption is about having the correct frame of mind to set something straight that may seem irreparably damaged. This is about taking the first step toward fixing the unfixable. This is about humbling ourselves. This is about meekness as our Savior defined it. This is about putting our pride and our world-supported egos on the shelf. This is about taking the Word of God to mean exactly what it says and, therefore, to *unconditionally refuse to sit in judgment of our wife*. This is about seeing our Savior's face in the face of our God-ordained life partner and humbling ourselves before her just exactly like He has requested.

It is also about truth. For there is an amazing thing about sin—even *little* sin. It always comes with a dose of blindness. This may be one of the top ten Biblical truths. It is literally scattered all through the Word of God.

> *I will bring distress on the people and they will walk like blind men, because they have sinned against the LORD.*
> —Zephaniah 1:17

When we sin, the power of the Holy Spirit is squelched in our lives. Without the Holy Spirit, we truly are blind. For only through His help can we see things as they really are, as God sees them.

So let's recognize the facts. If we have sinned against God in any way in our relationship with our wife, we may well be completely blind to it now. The hard truth is that most of us have sinned a lot in this most critical of relationships. The blindness is there. Believe me. That is why it is discussed in so many books of the Bible. The extraordinary Biblical prevalence of the topic of blindness to sin confirms the assertion that it is common to all of us. It logically follows, therefore, that if you don't think you are blind to your sin, then most likely you are *really* blind.

> *All a man's ways seem right to him, but the LORD weighs the heart.*
> —Proverbs 21:2

Let's recognize this right up front so we can deal with it. Only by bringing it out into the open do we have any chance of sidestepping its crippling effects.

Besides, how do you know that the assumption written above isn't true? How do you know it isn't exactly and completely true? How do you know that it does not describe your situation *perfectly*? When the Holy Spirit first put it on my heart, I had the same initial reaction, "Maybe it is partially true, but not totally."

But, as I have, by God's grace alone, humbled myself before my wife, I have seen her blossom magnificently and beautifully out of the cocoon within which *my* sin had wrapped her. I have come to realize more and more that it was *me* all along. Oh man, does that ever hurt. The truth gradually came to light as I began to realize that even the offenses she *had* committed in our relationship were mostly just in response to *my* transgressions.

Ouch.

Then, over the years, that which I had feared from the beginning—that it might actually be true, that I might be *totally* at fault—became incredibly and undeniably apparent, even to my very blind heart.

Now I have the most foundational of evidence that it was, indeed, entirely my fault. For now that Jesus has helped me change, lo and behold, my wife completely quit doing all of the things I had attributed to her as her contribution to the problem. Don't get me wrong. This did not occur overnight. It took awhile for all of the effects of my marriage-long bombardment of my wife to go away, but eventually they did. As soon as she came out from the defensive, bomb-shelter position that my actions had driven her to, and into the light that is our loving God, she blossomed back into the spectacular woman that she is. She is now, once again, the woman with whom I had first fallen so madly in love.

Bottom-line: my fault, *totally* my fault.

There is always considerable natural resistance to accepting this assumption and making it a part of our lives. This resistance is straight from Satan. It is something you can count on. Pushing back hard is what Satan does when hearts are surrendering to the will of God. This hard truth about our contribution to the problems in our marriage is the last thing in the world Satan wants us to believe. He fights it tooth-and-nail because that frame of mind, of humble repentance and submission to our wife, is the last thing in the world he wants us to be in when he tries to stir things up between us. More specifically, Satan knows that a heart humbled before God and before our wife is nothing short of God's awesome presence in our life. It is Jesus in command of our heart—we certainly can't do it without Him. A humbled servant's heart is undeniable evidence, therefore, that Jesus is in command of our heart. This humble servant's heart is our single best defense against the trickery with which Satan tries to convince us to disobey God in our daily interactions with our wife.

He guides the humble in what is right and teaches them his way.
—Psalm 25:9

But, oh how this little humbling assumption will change our life. This life change is a guarantee straight from the Word of God. It requires, however, nothing less than a single-minded, total commitment. The necessarily unconditional nature of this commitment once again gets back to the question of whether it is possible to humble oneself too much. Personally, you will never convince me that this is even a possibility. The Bible offers no examples of the occurrence of, or even the possibility of a human being humbling himself or herself too much. In fact, never in the Word of God are we even asked to be careful or cautious about this attitude of total servanthood. I know my life experience has reflected the eternal veracity of the Word of God in this regard. In every situation, the *more* I have humbled myself, the more God has raised me up.

> *He has brought down rulers from their thrones but has lifted up the humble.*
> —Luke 1:52

The call to unconditional servanthood is a clear-cut, unambiguous Biblical truth that most of us choose to simply look past. We allow ourselves the liberty of choosing which situations are worthy of our humbling ourselves—as if we, in our wisdom, can even make that call. We can be so blind at times. It is actually so much easier to just fully humble ourselves in *all* situations.

> *Though I am free and belong to no man, I make myself a slave to everyone, to win as many as possible.*
> —1Corinthians 9:19 (emphasis added)

The manifestations of the glory and true freedom of the kingdom of God find their greatest expression in our marriages only in this full and unconditional commitment to meekness.

> *For the LORD takes delight in his people; he crowns the humble with salvation.*
> —Psalm 149:4

In those rare circumstances in my life where I went to the very edge of the conceivable in my efforts to humble myself before my wife—I mean what I would have called *way out on the edge humbling*—God has done nothing less than glorious things in our marriage. Now, those circumstances—which I used to label as being incidents of extreme humbleness—somehow don't seem so extreme anymore.

Satan wants us to believe that humbling ourselves totally before our wife is a sign of weakness. The truth is quite the opposite. Totally humbling oneself is a sign of *extreme* power—God's power. In fact, it is a sign of *ultimate* power. Nothing is more powerful than great power willingly, submissively surrendered.

Copyright 2005 Michael K. Pasque

This is the very definition of meekness. This is all about Jesus Christ. Jesus reached the culmination of His power in His utter and absolute surrender of all power on the cross of Calvary. Truly, in His ultimate weakness was His ultimate power demonstrated.

> *That is why, for Christ's sake, I delight in weaknesses, in insults, in hardships, in persecutions, in difficulties. For when I am weak, then I am strong.*
>
> —2Corinthians 12:10

Jesus is our perfect model. His example is clear in regard to submitting to our wife. His example tells us that the ultimate consummation of our power as a husband can only be found in its supreme surrender.

Meekness in our marriage tells the whole world—and most importantly our wife—that we have made it to the *Majors*. We are playing in the *Big Leagues* now. We are doing things the way that God wants us to do them. It is a sign of nothing less than the activation of Almighty God's will and power in our lives. It is exactly what Jesus did on the cross and it is His command to us. Only when we are able to follow this command does He weigh into our life with the fullness of His grace, mercy and awesome power. When He does this, the very foundations of heaven—and of our marriage—are shaken with the richness of His glory.

Copyright 2005 Michael K. Pasque

Chapter 8

The Only Real Marriage Manual

<u>Assumption #8</u>
The only real marriage manual that you need is the Bible.

For most of us, it is readily apparent that getting and keeping our marriage on the right track requires a change in perspective. This is a radical change from the perspective that we have adopted from the world around us. This Christ-centered, eternity-based perspective is neither described nor condoned in secular publications on marriage. When our vision—our perspective—is impaired, we really can't seek help from a society that is blinder to reality than we are. Indeed, getting right with our wife is not about picking up one of the dozens of self-help relationship books that we see littering the shelves of secular bookstores. Not even the ones written by Christians. Not even the one you are reading. For the solution to our dilemma is not found in clichés and cutesy little tricks from the marriage manuals. It is not about figuring out what your wife's *personality type definition* might be or *99 different ways* to make your marriage better.

It is, plain and simple, about nothing less than the most important thing in life: our relationship with Jesus Christ.

For, as we have discussed, when we are in the proper relationship with our Creator, Savior, Lord and God, we will, by definition, be in the proper relationship with our wife.

This is an intriguing bit of circular logic that necessarily emanates from our previous discussion. It readily follows that if your relationship with your wife is a reflection, a barometer, of your relationship with your Savior, then the way to fix your relationship with your wife (a secondary issue) is to fix your relationship with God (the primary issue).

Truly we are led astray when we build marriage up into some secular icon that somehow exists separate from the knowledge of God. Marriage is all about God. He created the universe and He designed it that way. He created marriage as a *type* of our relationship with Jesus. If you want to fix your marriage, you have to fix your relationship with God. If you want to know how and why your wife thinks and acts the way she does, then you need to know how and why God thinks and acts the way He does. The only easily accessible, always there when you need it,

Copyright 2005 Michael K. Pasque

one reliable source for knowledge about how and why God thinks and acts the way He does is *the Bible*.

There simply is, therefore, no way to be in the proper relationship with our Lord and Creator (and therefore our wife) without being deep into the Word of God on a daily basis. We might as well not even try anything else. If we have not made reading the Bible a systematic priority in our every-day life, exactly as God tells us to, we will never know God *and we will never know our wife*. The word of God holds the key to our relationship with Jesus. It holds the key to our daily life and interaction with every person God brings us into contact with and, without a doubt, it contains every single bit of information we need to flourish in our relationship with our wife. It is complete in every respect. It is all encompassing in every respect. It, like its Author, has no deficiencies. It is the only pathway to developing and maintaining the proper perspective and presence of the Living God. In like kind, it is therefore the only pathway to developing and maintaining the correct relationship with our wife.

When I look back upon the course of my marriage, there is no question that the single point at which our relationship began to turn around seemingly had nothing to do with my wife. The change began many years ago. One day I decided that if I really believed that Jesus was exactly who He said He was, then this belief required a change in my life. By God's grace, I decided that day to set my alarm clock 20 minutes earlier so I could get to my office earlier. That next morning, for 20 minutes I closed my office door and devoted myself 100% to reading the Bible. My life changed from that day forward. Pretty soon I began to set my alarm 40 minutes earlier and then an hour earlier.

No other single factor so profoundly reversed the course of my marriage than this single decision to honor God and read His Holy Word.

The more I found out about God, the more I found out about my wife. The more I honored God, the more I found myself honoring my wife. The more I came to understand the mind of God, the more I came to understand her. It is not about you. It is not about me. It is not about her. It is not about marriage. It is—and for eternity will be—about God, and God alone. If we want to keep our marriage strong, we have to read His holy Word every day.

Copyright 2005 Michael K. Pasque

Chapter 9

What She Really Sees In You

Assumption #9
Deep in every woman's heart is the undeniable desire to be married to a man of God who runs hard after Jesus. If your marriage is in trouble, you're not running anymore.

In the heart of every woman is a divinely placed desire *to be married to a man of God*. This desire, more specifically, is an undeniable need to share her life with a man whose primary desire is to seek the face of Jesus Christ in every aspect of his life. The basis for this desire is that she, like her husband, has at the very center of her heart a God-designed void that can only be filled by the knowledge of God.

> *O God, you are my God, earnestly I seek you; my soul thirsts for you, my body longs for you, in a dry and weary land where there is no water. I have seen you in the sanctuary and beheld your power and your glory. Because your love is better than life, my lips will glorify you. I will praise you as long as I live, and in your name I will lift up my hands. My soul will be satisfied as with the richest of foods; with singing lips my mouth will praise you.*
>
> —Psalm 63:1-5

A woman's desire to be married to a man of God is in her wiring. It is in her very DNA—lovingly placed there by her Creator. The influence of this desire on her life is undeniable. She may try to ignore it. She may allow the lies of the world to cover it up so that this desire is no longer on the surface. She may seek similar fulfillment by many other avenues. But any efforts to gain satisfaction in a relationship with a man that are based upon his good looks, intelligence, wealth, fame or any characteristic other than his relationship with God are destined by the very Creator of the universe to fail.

Furthermore, her Creator has also defined the very nature of her desired relationship with that God-ordained man. Her deep heart desire is definitely not to be *the object* of that man's life. No matter how much Hollywood tries to convince her of this, it simply is not true. Any relationship based upon this desire is destined to fail. Why? Because, despite what the world may tell her, it's not about her. It's not about him. It is about God. If she has fully bought into the world's lies, she may believe that having a man doting over her every notion will make her happy. After all, that is the theme of most of the *chick-flicks* that come out of Hollywood these days. Their message is clear: true romance can only be found in a relationship with a man whose only desire is his woman. This Hollywood lie is in fact exactly what makes a chick-flick a chick-flick.

But reality, God's ordained reality, just does not play out that way. Think of any couple you have known who had a relationship based primarily upon the guy's doting, fawning, single burning desire to please his woman. It may be okay for a bit, but not for long. This is not the stuff of long-lasting relationships.

Why not? Let's take this thought process one step further. Would God—could God—allow that to happen? Would He allow you, or any of His created beings for that matter, to find complete, permanent satisfaction in any thing or person other than Himself? If you think logically about the known attributes of God, it is not long before you realize that if He could even allow it to happen that way, then He wouldn't be God. If the objects of His desire that He created could find complete and permanent satisfaction in anything other than Him, then He wouldn't be God—by definition. God is all encompassing, awesomely righteous, and perfectly infinite in every respect—including the depth of His love. By definition, there can be no desire in His created beings that circumvents their desire for Him.

The bottom-line: Hollywood is wrong. Our wife should not be the focus of our life. Likewise, the focus of her life should not be to maintain our doting attention. That is not the way either of us is designed.

Instead, God designed her to want to spend her life with a man of God, a man who seeks God in everything. She doesn't want to be the object of that man's attention because deep down in her wiring burns the very same passion that drives his life—to know God. She wants a guy to be her partner on the grand adventure that God has placed before her, but she does not want *to be* that grand adventure. Deep in her heart she knows there is something more, something awesome out there; something entirely outside of herself; something entirely outside of her husband; something bigger than the both of them. She wants to share the quest for that something with a man of God. She doesn't want a guy who is focused only on her. That type of relationship is a dead-end street that leads nowhere. She wants a guy who is focused on God.

Do you want to keep your wife interested in you? Do you want to get her attention or keep her attention? Then get your nose in the Word of God. Set your

Copyright 2005 Michael K. Pasque

mind on obeying God. Set your heart on chasing hard after Jesus and seeking His face in every moment of every activity of your every day. Pray hard. Work hard toward the goal of your sanctification—to be transformed into the image of Jesus Christ. *His* is the face she seeks. *His* is the face whose image is emblazoned on her heart:

> *My heart says of you, "Seek his face!" Your face, LORD, I will seek.*
> —Psalm 27:8

The more you resemble Jesus in your thoughts, words, and actions, the more you will appeal to her, because He is who she *really* seeks.

If you are running hard after God, you will be irresistible to her. She won't be able to help herself. She may not even understand why she is so attracted to you. She may even struggle with this attraction since most women seem to have bought into the lies the world is trying to pass off as reality. But she will come around. Her heart's desire, whether she will admit it or not, is Jesus Christ.

> *My soul yearns, even faints, for the courts of the LORD; my heart and my flesh cry out for the living God.*
> —Psalm 84:2

His Name is above all names and He is the focus of—very simply put—*everything*. She may deny it, but she simply has no choice in the way she is designed. She is not empowered to rewrite the script that was written on her heart by the hand of God. She does, indeed, have the God-ordained, God-guarded authority to refuse God. She may, in fact, choose to turn her back on Him, but that will not change anything. Her heart's desire will still be to seek the face of God.

> *Whom have I in heaven but you? And earth has nothing I desire besides you.*
> —Psalm 73:25

She will get excited about you because you are excited about God, plain and simple. What will really turn her head is the perception that not only is your heart's desire for God, but that you are on target in your quest. She doesn't want to be left out. She is just like the rest of us. She doesn't want to miss out on her heart's desire. Nothing will light her up like the perception that you have your will focused precisely on God's will, that you know where the answers can be found (the Word of God), and that you are *hot on the trail*. By nothing less than God's precise design, this perception is exactly what makes you the kind of exciting life partner

Copyright 2005 Michael K. Pasque

she wants to join in the quest. You become like a mirror reflecting what she, in the deepest reaches of her heart, wants to gaze at for eternity.

In other words, what makes you exciting in her eyes—what makes you absolutely irresistible—is that you know exactly what you are doing and exactly *whom* you are seeking. This tells her that you know exactly what this life, this adventure, is all about. She is designed, once again not by her will or choice, to desire a partner in her life adventure. You share that desire. This is also by God's design. Exactly because it is His design, the adventure that you share will be more fulfilling because you both seek the face of God *together*. She wants someone to go before her into battle. She wants you to cover her back and she wants to cover yours. She wants to team with you to make sure she gets what she knows is her heart's desire.

Of equal importance, this also applies to you. Your heart's desire is to seek the only real goal of life, Jesus, *with* a woman of God. Deep down in the dark, quiet places of our manly hearts, where we don't often venture, is an intense God-instilled fascination with a woman who walks with God.

Charm is deceptive, and beauty is fleeting; but a woman who fears the LORD is to be praised.

—Proverbs 31:30

You know this is true. You need that. I need that. We, just like them, were designed to take this trip *with* somebody. We were designed to travel the great quest, the great adventure that is *life*, as partners who fill in the blank spots on each other's maps. We each need a partner who has the survival skill-set that we lack, a partner who picks up the ball when we drop it. We all need a partner who can lead when we can't and a partner who will let us lead when it is our turn, when it is our time, and when our special gifts are needed.

We, like they, can deny this need all we want. We can believe we exist as an island, a self-sufficient force on a mission. The world would try to convince us of this in the movies we see, the books we read, and the heroes we worship. But, the facts are clear. That is not the way our Creator designed us, or our partner, or this whole adventure that we share. We need them. They need us. We are part of a team whether we like it or not. We need fellowship on the journey whether we think so or not. And we especially need the very special fellowship found in the tripartite relationship of marriage the way God planned it—Jesus dead center in the middle of a God-ordained fellowship between a man and a woman.

Indeed, the combination of a man of God with a woman of God is not merely additive in its benefit to both. This combination increases the knowledge of God that is available to both in an *exponential* fashion. There is much to be gained by acknowledging God's sovereignty in this and proceeding in the manner *He* has prescribed.

And once again, as in all things, the true focus, the whole point of the whole thing, is Jesus Christ. The truths about relationships and about life that the Word of God teaches are manifest in this fact.

> *But seek first his kingdom and his righteousness, and all these things will be given to you as well.*
>
> —Matthew 6:33

We can therefore be assured that if we seek satisfaction by seeking each other, by making each other the object of our lives, we will find neither satisfaction nor each other. In a similar fashion, if we seek to prioritize our relationship with each other on the same level as our priority for seeking God, then we will find neither each other nor God. In seeking Jesus as the single priority on a list of priorities that has only one priority listed, we will find Jesus—*and* we will find each other. If we seek the face of God *together*, as a team designated before time by God for this express purpose, we will find both God and each other to the ultimate God-ordained degree.

Copyright 2005 Michael K. Pasque

Chapter 10

Doing Things Against Her Will

Assumption #10
There can be no excuse for doing things against her will.

Anyone who has lived the day-to-day life of a Christian marriage knows that some of the biggest problems we face arise from seemingly innocuous everyday decisions. In possibly no other situation, however, is the warning that *the devil is in the details* more applicable. If you have been married for any length of time, then you know what I am describing. Marital problems seem to most often arise as a result of simple differences of opinion that do not appear to involve a choice between right and wrong. Instead, these are most often just simple family decisions regarding everyday choices about which our wife and we happen to have differing opinions. For instance, we may want to move ahead with a special home project and our wife doesn't. We may think we can't afford something that she wants to buy. She may want to visit her family during this year's vacation time and we don't. These are basically just differing opinions on choices that face the family unit. But how often these seemingly simple choices turn into major disagreements that plague our relationships!

It is critically important that we look at this problem with the proper perspective—in other words, through *eternal* eyes. Let's make this personal. Let's talk about you. Try to focus, for a moment, on a recent controversial decision you and your wife have faced together. Even at first glance, it is readily apparent that the very reason issues like these keep coming up is because she was chosen precisely for you. In fact, she was selected as your life mate for her exact response to this exact set of circumstances. We truly are naïve if we believe that this is all just a random bit of happenstance in our lives. God knew both of your choices in this set of circumstances before time began. He planned the whole thing. His divine will set the whole thing in motion. He wants desperately to teach you something here. Worst of all, you can be guaranteed that if you don't learn it this time around, He already has another backup lesson planned for you. A simple difference of opinion like this one should therefore ring the *school's-in-session* bell—instead of triggering an argument.

Copyright 2005 Michael K. Pasque

My failure to grasp the concept that God was trying to instruct me in these situations was one of the biggest stumbling blocks in our marriage. I missed on this one so many times it isn't even funny. God had many lessons to teach me and was not going to let me out of school without an A+. Let me give you an example from my recent experience to see if you can relate it to your marriage. Actually, I am sure you will be able to relate, because I'm convinced that our lessons are all very similar as God tries to lead each of us to one final common pathway, resembling one person—His Son, Jesus.

I am not saying we aren't individuals. The Word of God clearly teaches that our individuality is highly cherished and strictly guarded by our God and Creator. But regarding our character and our integrity, our sanctification process has one common, final pathway under the Father's close scrutiny. The goal of that pathway is the very character and integrity of Jesus Christ. If we are all reasonably similar to begin with and if the final product is the same, the lessons are going to have to be pretty similar. That is why I would love to hear your stories, too. I have no doubt we could all learn from them.

My example stems from my recent desire to finish our basement. I am so ready to get this done. It's a cold, dark mess down there and I want to transform it into a more functional part of the house. I want to refinish it into an area our family can expand into—especially as an area in which our kids can have an abundance of space to play. It's a reasonable venture—in my eyes. We have saved up the money to do it now, so money isn't an issue like it often is. We have both agreed that we want to get it finished and we have both agreed on what it will look like. We have a contractor who we both like, who is now telling us he has an opening coming up during which he could fit us in and get it completed.

I am a project guy. I am a *get it done* guy. Odds are, you are too. I think it is pretty much in the male wiring. Needless to say, I am ready to get going.

My wife, unfortunately, has allergies. She is convinced—and I am sure she is right—that construction, with all the dust and stuff, really aggravates her condition. She has just come off a pretty rowdy time with her allergies and she simply does not want to risk another big flare-up. Period.

Well, that may or may not be reasonable. After all, everything has come together and everybody is ready to proceed except her. One might be tempted to invoke the old *leader of the Christian home* theology and simply overrule her decision. After all, you might be thinking, didn't God lay that out fairly plainly in Ephesians?

> *Wives, submit to your husbands as to the Lord. For the husband is the head of the wife as Christ is the head of the church, his body, of which*

Copyright 2005 Michael K. Pasque

he is the Savior. Now as the church submits to Christ, so also wives should submit to their husbands in everything.
—Ephesians 5:22-24

This must be the single most overachieving scripture in the New Testament. It probably gets quoted more in situations where it simply does not apply than any other scripture.

In fact, nothing could be further from God's will than to have husbands *"lording it over"* (1Peter 5:3) their wife the way many Christian men believe this scripture justifies. Isn't God's will precisely what this is all about, putting ourselves dead center in the middle of His will for our lives? I know it is the cry of my heart and I know it is the cry of your heart also. Our main objective must be, therefore, to figure out on an event-by-event basis, just exactly what God wants us to do. In this regard, we know that God has set these precise events against us to grow us. We just have to figure out what our response should be. We don't want to know about the bare minimum response that will get us a passing grade. We don't want to *just get by*. We want to know what the A+ response is. This is what knowing His will in our life is all about. The single greatest source of information regarding our response to every event of our every day is the written Word of God. It is there that we are told that it is not okay to overrule our wife in this, or any other similar set of circumstances.

"Whoa there! Never overrule your wife? Are you kidding?"

There is no doubt that it is sometimes very difficult for me to sort out all the events of my day in regard to God's will.

But this is not one of those circumstances.

It is never okay for me to make my wife miserable or to raise myself above her in any such decision-making process. Never. God's command is to love her, to put her desires above my own, not just when it is convenient for me, but every time. Exactly when it looks like putting her desires above mine is illogical, is going to be incredibly difficult, and poses as a major nuisance, is the exact time that this most applies. It is in these exact circumstances that I am to love her and trust God to take care of the consequences. It is in these exact circumstances that I am most sure that I am to bow in humble servanthood to my wife.

These difficult situations are all about one thing: trusting God. The scenario is always the same. God as told us what kind of behavior pleases Him. He orchestrates circumstances in our lives that then require us to make a choice. It is either His way or the world's way. Satan is there to try to convince us that it will be a disaster if we do it God's way. The Holy Spirit is there to tell us to choose God and to trust God to take care of the consequences. It is the same scenario in every decision in our lives and the answer is always the same. This holds true even

Copyright 2005 Michael K. Pasque

in our most trying encounters with our wife—especially in our most trying encounters with our wife. What an abomination it is to force a decision upon our wife *in the name of God* using our *headship* of the family as our excuse to get our way. How can that ever be God's will for our lives?

Those who interpret the scripture above as saying that the husband, as the head of the house, can run roughshod over his wife's desires are sadly mistaken. That scripture has nothing to do with giving a man the ability to dominate his wife in the decisions they make for their families. No way. Read it again. Especially read the lines that follow it.

> *Husbands, love your wives, just as Christ loved the church and gave himself up for her to make her holy, cleansing her by the washing with water through the word, and to present her to himself as a radiant church, without stain or wrinkle or any other blemish, but holy and blameless. In this same way, husbands ought to love their wives as their own bodies. He who loves his wife loves himself. After all, no one ever hated his own body, but he feeds and cares for it, just as Christ does the church—for we are members of his body.*
>
> *"For this reason a man will leave his father and mother and be united to his wife, and the two will become one flesh." This is a profound mystery—but I am talking about Christ and the church. However, each one of you also must love his wife as he loves himself, and the wife must respect her husband.*
>
> —Ephesians 5:25-33

We are to serve our wife like Jesus served His bride, the Church. His example in regard to *His* bride is stark in its clarity. He simply could not have humbled Himself any more than He did for the redeemed Church.

> *Your attitude should be the same as that of Christ Jesus: Who, being in very nature God, did not consider equality with God something to be grasped, but made himself nothing, taking the very nature of a servant, being made in human likeness. And being found in appearance as a man, he humbled himself and became obedient to death—even death on a cross!*
>
> —Philippians 2:5-8

God became man and allowed the beings He created to spit on Him and murder Him so that He could save them for all eternity. That is, and will always

Copyright 2005 Michael K. Pasque

remain, the single greatest event of *humbling oneself* in all recorded history. The greatness of an act of humbling oneself can only be determined by the distance one has voluntarily fallen in that act—and there can be no greater distance that that which separates the holy, uncreated God from sinful man. Jesus is our perfect example of how we are to live. He is the only measure against which we will be judged. Clearly, His intention is that we are to mirror His response to these exact circumstances and to humble ourselves before our bride just like He did—to humble ourselves totally.

I am utterly convicted by the example of Jesus Christ. The God-ordained manner in which we are to lead our family is to bow humbly before them, to hold nothing back, to serve them, to wash their feet, to give them our very lives.

> *Greater love has no one than this, that he lay down his life for his friends.*
> —John 15:13

Truly, Jesus was the perfect example. He gave His life, very literally, for His bride. We are to do the same. Not to actually die for her—that's too easy. Instead, we are to do something that is far more difficult than actually dying. We are to give up our life for her every day—in the small things. We are to take on the incredible task of serving her in *all* circumstances. We are to *die to ourselves* so that we can focus on Jesus and in so doing, focus on her. Simply put, we are to put her desires above ours every single day. We are to prioritize her wishes above ours—no matter how unreasonable they may seem to us.

> *This is how we know what love is: Jesus Christ laid down his life for us. And we ought to lay down our lives for our brothers.*
> —1John 3:16

This is, of course, excluding sin. We are never to give in where sin is involved. But let's not get distracted here. We are not talking about her sin in 99% of these contentious issues. We are talking about the things that we have disagreements about on a daily basis—little things that somehow get so wildly blown out of proportion in our day-to-day interactions.

Let's get back to my situation. I freely admit I can't discern the will of God in my life in every set of circumstances that confront me every day. But, I know exactly what it is in this one. There is no way in the world that it is God's will for my life that I should raise myself and my priorities and desires above hers—that I should say to her, "Your fears are not reasonable and should not delay the remodeling of our basement."

Copyright 2005 Michael K. Pasque

This is the lesson I am to learn from this example. Again and again, I am to humble myself before my lovely, God-decreed wife and seek her will over mine in every circumstance where it becomes an issue. In doing exactly this, I place my trust in God and His willingness and ability to make things okay, to fix the problems. In doing this, I unleash God's power in my marriage. I empower *His* will in my family. To make my wife unhappy, anxious, fearful, or sick because I happen to think it is best for the family is nothing less than true and total blindness. Total blindness to the Word of God and, therefore, to the will of God in my life. The word of God in this regard is crystal clear.

Submit to one another out of reverence for Christ.
—Ephesians 5:21

So how about you? I know you have faced similar decisions—and may be facing one right now. I hope the Word of God convicts you that it is never okay to raise yourself above your bride. God expects us to be perfect in our obedience. He doesn't want us to pick and choose when and where we will humble ourselves before our wife. He doesn't want us to *think* and use our worldly *wisdom* regarding when and where and in which circumstances we should obey Him. He just wants us to obey and humble ourselves every time. He wants us to be perfect in this.

As a prisoner for the Lord, then, I urge you to live a life worthy of the calling you have received. Be completely humble and gentle; be patient, bearing with one another in love.
—Ephesians 4:1-2

The most awesome part of all this is the perfect faithfulness of God. When we choose to honor Him by obeying Him, He will often act mightily in our immediate circumstances. He may even change her mind. After all, if she has given her life to our Lord, He has her ear too. He can change her heart in a heartbeat. And He does—very often. If, on the other hand, she is not a Christian, then we are to be a witness to her and the last thing a witness of the love of Jesus Christ would do is force his will upon his wife in such a manner. She will simply look at him and say, "I sure don't want any of that in my life. He is a 'Believer' and he is a total jerk."

It is, therefore, my unchangeable rule that I will never proceed with a project, an investment, a purchase, or a family direction—without the complete and total assent of my beloved. Period. If God wants us to go in the direction that my great "wisdom" has discerned, then I can rest in complete confidence that He will similarly enlighten the mind of my life partner. There are very few absolute

Copyright 2005 Michael K. Pasque

rules, but that is a pretty good one. Every time I have been tempted to break it, when I just knew my wife was not on track, God has shown *me* the light. So far in my life, the rule holds up. How about yours?

God has promised He will never abandon us. He has promised He will always be there and that He never sleeps and will never take His eyes off of us.

> *But the Lord stood at my side and gave me strength…*
> —2Timothy 4:17

God is watching. He always knows exactly what is going on. He always knows our hearts. We just need to trust Him in this circumstance—and in every circumstance—and do it His way. He will be there for us. And it will be total victory, the total victory that is found only in the knowledge of the Living God.

Copyright 2005 Michael K. Pasque

Chapter 11

Choose to Lose

<u>Assumption #11</u>
There is no fight that you can't stop.

The facts regarding fights are clear. Fights require two opposing parties. If either side gives in, except in extraordinary situations, the fight is over. There is no denying this hard reality of conflict. Each one of us has, within our power as individual participants, the ability to end or continue any argument. In fact, we have the power to end or continue any fight, any siege, any feud, or any disagreement. It doesn't matter whether it is with our boss, our coworker, our child, our friend, our enemy, or our wife. It is almost as if this ability is a God-granted gift, right, or responsibility. We can stop any fight. The old adage that it *takes two to tango* certainly applies here. We can stop any fight.

How? You know how. We all know how.

Just surrender.

Surrender—one word the whole world, and our society in particular, just hates to say. *Surrender* is the equivalent of *lose* and nobody likes to lose. To voluntarily lose is a pathway that just makes no sense by any worldly standard. To the contrary, *the fight* is the glamorized choice in our society. Believe me, I know. I have always been a fighter. Fighting is the rewarded choice in this world. To the best fighters go the medals, the trophies, the acclaim, the honor, and the wealth. I love a fighter. You love a fighter. The entire world loves a fighter.

Just when the world has us convinced that something is unquestionably the goal, our awesome God steps in. Isn't it just like Him to ask us to surrender when the world says to fight? Isn't it just like God to use our relationship with our wife to reveal the foolishness of the wisdom of the world and the eternal glory of the knowledge of God?

> *For it is written: "I will destroy the wisdom of the wise; the intelligence of the intelligent I will frustrate." Where is the wise man? Where is the scholar? Where is the philosopher of this age? Has not God made foolish the wisdom of the world?*
>
> —1 Corinthians 1:19-20

Copyright 2005 Michael K. Pasque

Flying in the face of this worldly wisdom is exactly what God wants us to do. He doesn't want us to fight. He wants us to surrender. He wants us to do our part—to love the unlovable at their most unlovable moment in the most inopportune setting at the most critical time. At that exact moment, in the middle of a heated discussion when we are running on raw emotion instead of godly wisdom, when our minds no longer function rationally, is when He wants us to love *the enemy* that we have made our wife out to be. He wants us to surrender. He wants us to choose to lose. For it is precisely in our surrender to God and to man that God's awesome power is unleashed in our lives. When we surrender, He steps in. It is as if the appearance of our white flag of surrender is the exact cue for which His legions of angels are patiently waiting!

We hear a lot about surrendering our lives to God. What exactly does that mean? It is easy to say, hard to understand, and even harder to do. The difficulty arises as it becomes readily apparent from the reading of God's Word that the way we surrender to God is to surrender to man. In this case that means surrendering to our wife. For, as we have reviewed, to love Jesus we must obey Him (1John 5:3) and His command, from His very lips, is to *"love each other"* (John 15:17).

Loving each other means surrendering to each other, becoming servants to each other, placing our wife's needs and desires above our own. Jesus didn't just tell us to love each other by becoming servants and placing the needs of others above ours. Instead, it is exactly what He did in the greatest demonstration of love in recorded history, as God became man and died for our sins. We as mortal humans can never fully understand or appreciate the depth of the servanthood, the meekness, and the love for the Father that would prompt the eternal Son of the Living God to surrender and submit to such humiliation.

> *Jesus called them together and said, "You know that the rulers of the Gentiles lord it over them, and their high officials exercise authority over them. Not so with you. Instead, whoever wants to become great among you must be your servant, and whoever wants to be first must be your slave—just as the Son of Man did not come to be served, but to serve, and to give his life as a ransom for many."*
> —Matthew 20:25-28

Surrender to God is fulfilled almost entirely in our surrender to man—surrendering to the *enemies* He brings before us—surrendering specifically, in this case, to our wife.

Even so, God always gives us the choice. We can choose to do it our way. We can choose to fight. Unfortunately, the choice to fight takes God out of the discussion altogether. It sidelines the only One who can save the day. The whole of creation is designed that way: the only real, lasting and good solution to any problem is Jesus Christ. If we choose to sideline God, then we stand unassisted, face to face with Satan, the deceiver who has been turned loose on the world. I've been there many times. I'm sure you have too. I don't want to go there ever again.

In the midst of every one of these tumultuous times, however, there exists a once-in-a-lifetime opportunity to bring glory to God. For in each circumstance, God always gives us a way out. His Spirit is faithful to show us His pathway and Jesus is faithful to supply the grace we need to make the right decision.

No temptation has seized you except what is common to man. And God is faithful; he will not let you be tempted beyond what you can bear. But when you are tempted, he will also provide a way out so that you can stand up under it.
—1Corinthians 10:13

But he said to me, "My grace is sufficient for you…"
—2Corinthians 12:9

In our marital relationships, we never seem to choose God's way the first time around (or in my case, the first hundred times). The result is predictable: we get hammered. Then we look for another way. Some of us really hardheaded husbands take a bit longer, but eventually we go to the Lord and ask His Son to fill our hearts. We ask Him to give us His will and His strength to make the right choice. Only in heartfelt, full surrender to the servanthood of Christ do we find the answer. For it is in our surrender that we make ourselves weak and it is in our weakness that we are strong. Only in surrender and in weakness do we become like Jesus, the Creator of everything, hanging on the sacrificial cross of Calvary. Paul says it best.

To keep me from becoming conceited because of these surpassingly great revelations, there was given me a thorn in my flesh, a messenger of Satan, to torment me. Three times I pleaded with the Lord to take it away from me. But he said to me, "My grace is sufficient for you, for my power is made perfect in weakness." Therefore I will boast all the more gladly about my weaknesses, so that Christ's power may rest on me. That is why, for Christ's sake, I delight in weaknesses, in insults, in hardships, in persecutions, in difficulties. For when I am weak, then I am strong.
—2 Corinthians 12:7-10 (emphasis added)

Copyright 2005 Michael K. Pasque

A couple of qualifications are applicable to this discussion. Don't get me wrong. We should not submit to our wife when doing so stands in opposition to the knowledge of God as revealed in the Holy Scriptures. As we have discussed, never should our surrendering be seen as condoning sin. We should stand up for the Name of Jesus Christ and in defense of His Holy Word—always and every time.

But we have to be really careful here.

In the overwhelming majority of times—the overwhelming majority of times—surrender is clearly the correct course. We in our hearts know this full well. The choice to raise ourselves above our wife in a self-righteous stand can be a short step onto a very slippery slope.

By God's precise planning, real leadership and genuine authority are always founded in servanthood and the very mettle of servanthood is surrender. That is exactly the way God, in His perfect and pure wisdom, has designed this world and the people in it. To lead our families, *we serve*—just like Jesus served His apostles, His bride (the church), and all mankind. This means serving our wife to the extreme and thereby empowering God in our families. This means surrendering to her just like Jesus surrendered to the will of the Father by surrendering to the will of men. The Father took care of everything then by the glorious resurrection of Jesus. He will take care of our problems, too.

We can be assured that we really can't go too far in this surrender mode. Even in the worst of situations, God promises He will never leave us.

> *No one will be able to stand up against you all the days of your life. As I was with Moses, so I will be with you; I will never leave you nor forsake you.*
>
> —Joshua 1:5

If we truly humble ourselves *in His Name* by surrendering to our wife, do you think there is any chance He will abandon us? No way. He always knows our true heart. He always knows when we are trying to be the peacemaker rather than propagating a fight. He knows our intentions. He will never abandon us. We can be assured of this. That certainly was always the truth in the trials described in Old Testament Scripture. There was never a battle too big, a foe too powerful, a situation too scary for God to handle. We can be assured that if our hearts are emptied humbly before our God, He will follow us into any situation in which we are led by the Spirit to surrender.

So, let's choose to lose in every fight, every *situation* that we find ourselves in with our wife. Even when we have been ambushed and have responded poorly, we can still save the day. We can turn our backs on our pride, for truly this is

Copyright 2005 Michael K. Pasque

always an issue of pride. We can turn our backs on our egos. We can turn our backs on the world and all of its so-called *wisdom*. We can humble ourselves and throw ourselves on the mercy of our perfectly merciful God. We can say to our wife, right in the middle of the heated discussion, "Wait, I'm sorry. I was wrong. I made a mistake. I should not have responded to your request that way."

You don't need me to tell you that surrender is right in every situation. You've already been there, and you know it in your heart—just like I know it in mine. The facts are that in every single disagreement, God has given us the ability to simply stop the fight cold—the ability *and the responsibility*. This option is always there. The ability to stop the fight exists in every single second of every single minute of every single fight we have with our wife. It is always there and it is always the right answer, no matter how far down the fight path we may have gone. At the beginning of the fight, in the middle of the fight, and even at the end of the fight, unconditional surrender will always work. It is the God-given, get-out-of-trouble card that can be played any time and that trumps everything else. What a gift. What a responsibility. What a God!

My recent life is a litany of examples and I can tell you that *real-life* surrendering works. God is perfectly faithful to His promises. It stops the *discussion* cold when I surrender. And then the Lord really goes to work. Then, and only then, I get to see the awesome power of the Living God. In literally every situation He has warmed the heart of my *opponent* and allowed the argument to stop immediately. My wife loves it. She loves the Lord and when I abruptly stop a disagreement with an apology and a major league turn toward a humble heart, she feels embarrassed and hugs me immediately. That is the power of Almighty God unleashed mightily in my life. I get to watch Him melt the ice in her heart. Suddenly, this big important point that each of us was trying to make now seems so very unimportant. We hug and we feel so silly to have let things move down that path. Sometimes she beats me to the punch with *her* unconditional surrender—even when I'm at fault! What a God.

So, I challenge you. Try it if you haven't already. Put God to this test. He loves it. Then step back and watch Him do His work. It's awesome. With every fight you find yourself in, remember that Jesus offers nothing less than a ringside seat for an awesome display of the breathtaking power of the Creator of the Universe.

Copyright 2005 Michael K. Pasque

Chapter 12

Forgiving is Foundational

<u>Assumption #12</u>
Unconditional forgiveness, characterized by willful forgetting of her offenses, must rule your relationship with your wife.

Learning to forgive is the very foundation of loving our wife and of actively nourishing this most significant of relationships. The significance of forgiveness in any healthy marriage is firmly established by the fact that in any close relationship, mistakes will be made. Offenses will be committed. These offenses cannot help but stand as major stumbling blocks in our marriages unless they are unconditionally forgiven.

You may be saying to yourself that you really don't have any trouble forgiving your wife. If you are anything like me, your confidence in this regard may be a bit overstated. Let's start this discussion by contemplating a few revealing questions. Think about a recent disagreement you have had with your wife. Recall your feelings about how she treated you. Have you forgiven her for that? How do you know you have truly forgiven her? What criteria do you use to confirm that assertion? Do any of your actions suggest otherwise?

It is critical that we be honest with ourselves when answering these key questions. The facts remain that truly forgiving our wife is one of the toughest things we are asked to do. The times in our relationship when true forgiveness is needed are always the times when we are most vulnerable to fooling ourselves regarding our heart's true commitment. I can't tell you how many times husbands have assured me that they have forgiven their wife for a specific offense, only to have their actions reveal there really is no forgiveness at all. My track record on this is not exactly stellar either. I have repeatedly spoken of forgiveness in my relationship with my wife, only to have my actions all too clearly reveal the true level of my commitment to this direct command from Jesus.

So, what does true forgiveness really look like? Let's start from the very foundation of this issue. Simply put, forgiving is *forgetting*. I know that sounds trite. We've all heard the old saying: *forgive and forget*. But, the facts remain, forgiving really is all about forgetting. In fact, we can practically define true forgiveness as the active, volitional form of forgetting another person's offenses.

Not mindless forgetful forgetting like we all do every day—but rather voluntary, willful forgetting. Willful forgetting means that when her offenses come to mind, we choose to not dwell on them. We willfully choose to move on in our thoughts to other issues—anything that is good and loving and godly regarding our wife and our relationship with her. We have to want to move on. We have to will to forget, we have to want to forget, in order to truly forgive.

And that is exactly how we do it in our marriage relationship. We have to want to let go of the offenses committed by our wife that have hurt us. Permanently. That is how we forget and is what really forgiving our wife is all about.

Sounds easy you say? Try it. Think of something your wife (or anyone else for that matter) has done to you that you are really having trouble just *letting go of*. Now, try to forget it. Imagine forgetting it—really forgetting it. Imagine that your memory of that particular offense is no longer retrievable. Imagine that offense no longer being available for you to dredge up when you need it (especially in a moment of duress) to dwell upon, to use as a weapon, or to fuel so-called *righteous* anger. Imagine it no longer being available to you during your little "woe is me" pity-parties. Imagine it no longer being available for you to hold against her *ever* again.

Let's be honest here. It is hard to permanently let go, isn't it? We are naturally resistant to the finality of permanently and irrevocably giving up the memory of any enemy's offenses against us. It almost hurts to really forgive someone. This is why we don't forgive as often as we should. After all, someone has inflicted pain upon us. They *deserve* to hurt as much as we have been hurt. Forgiving them—letting them off the hook without inflicting a similar degree of pain—means, very simply, that the score has not been settled. By God's design, a price still has to be paid—and when we choose to forgive, we pay that price. This is why truly letting go of the resentment and anger wounds us deep in our hearts. God designed it this way.

Precisely this is the message of the cross of Christ. For true forgiveness to occur, *someone* must pay a very real price. Every one of us has rebelliously sinned against God. In doing so, we have inflicted injury upon the heart of God. Justice demands that an equal injury be meted back. We simply cannot get out from under this debt without a price being paid. *Someone* has to pay the price. Otherwise, that which is demanded by God's perfect justice—eternal death—is our only possible destiny. We have no way to pay that price, so Jesus went to the cross to do precisely that—to suffer that which is demanded by true forgiveness. In a similar fashion, when we willfully forget our wife's offenses, when we forgive her, *we* pay that price. We mirror Jesus in this most noble of actions—suffering for someone who has willfully hurt us. This is foundation of the gospel of Jesus Christ.

Copyright 2005 Michael K. Pasque

The pain that we feel in this act of voluntary forgiving is precisely why we want so very badly to hold on to these thoughts, these memories of her offenses. It hurts to forgive and therefore holding on to her offenses seems somehow self-protective, self-preserving. Alternatively, if we are in Christ, *He* can forgive her for us. I am convinced that He is in fact the only source of true heart forgiveness. He is the font, the source, the Master of forgiveness. He defined it, wrote the book on it, and then demonstrated it Himself in the crowning act of forgiveness from which all others spring. The key to tapping into this source of forgiveness is the surrender of the kingship of our heart to its true King, Jesus. If we can just turn over the reigns of our heart to Jesus in the midst of these very difficult times, He promises to help us forgive. Once again, it is all about Him. It is always about Jesus—in everything, always—but especially in forgiveness. Forgiveness is what He is all about.

Dwelling on the memories of our wife's offenses against us can be addicting. We especially dwell on them during difficult times. They are the tiny specks of dust upon which we build giant crystals of hate. This is why even seemingly little offenses—combined with our refusal to really forgive them and forget them—can very literally be the beginning of the end of our marriage. They can be the tiny monkey wrench we naïvely toss into the delicate machinery of our marriage relationship that brings the gears to a grinding halt. For it is a very short step from just harmlessly thinking about these offenses to truly dwelling on them. Dwelling quickly leads to brooding. And it is brooding on them that is a very short slide to thoughts of retribution—thoughts and plans of exactly what we are going to do the next time she *tries something like that!*

> *All of us also lived among them at one time, gratifying the cravings of our sinful nature and following its desires and thoughts. Like the rest, we were by nature objects of wrath.*
>
> —Ephesians 2:3

Let's try a little test. Let's imagine giving that offense of hers—the one that really hurt us—to our Savior and asking Him to *make* us forget it. Let's ask Him to irretrievably remove it from our minds forever. Did you catch that? We are asking God to *actually do it*, to irrevocably take the memory of her offense from our minds—forever. We ask this with the full knowledge that He can and will do exactly what we ask. This is critical. We must want, ask, and beg our Savior to actually drive the thought from our mind forever, relying only on the power of His victory on the cross. Can you do that?

This is difficult stuff. I would nonetheless propose to you that this is the only way for us to get past our wife's offenses. The glaring facts are straightforward and simple: it is impossible for us to forget these offenses by ourselves. We are simply incapable of completing this critical task on our own. It is impossible because without the direct intervention of God—mediated directly through the cross of Christ—Satan can easily throw these thoughts about our wife's offenses right back into our mind. Satan knows that for most of us, this is all that it takes to start us down the wrong thought pathway yet again. He wants strife in our relationship with our wife. He also knows that a marriage relationship characterized by a lack of forgiveness is one that is ripe for his dark intervention. When we refuse to forgive we are maximally susceptible to Satan's temptation because our sin has blinded us to reality. He knows if he can just get us to start thinking about how she has hurt us, then off we go with plotting, scheming, anger, and hate.

Jesus offers us an alternative solution, just as He does to every problem in our life. Only He can truly change our deep heart. This is why we need the very God of all creation actually in our heart. This is why we must surrender our heart to Him. It is only in the surrendered heart that His will and our will become one. We can't forget her offense, but He can.

We can and must do our part in this transaction. We have to take the first step. God won't act in our heart and in our mind without our permission. He won't force us to forget our wife's offenses. We have to ask Him. We must take our wife's most grievous offenses and dump them right at the foot of the cross of Jesus Christ. His cross, His sacrifice, His strength, and His grace are the only solution to this problem, just as they are the only real solution to every problem we face. Every time those thoughts of our wife's offenses *are* thrown into our mind we need to grab them immediately, yet again, and throw them right to the foot of the cross. There the battle has been fought and the victory already won.

We must be committed to repeat this process as many times as is necessary. That is our part. It is that *perseverance* issue yet again. Jesus may—in His perfectly wise, divine will for our lives—not take her offenses immediately from our memory. The timing of their removal is always His to determine. We take the first step by asking Him to remove them, by giving Him permission to change our heart and mind. Then we must rely on His strength to help us grab them and throw them out of our minds every time Satan throws them in—until Jesus permanently binds their memory from our heart. He will do exactly that, but often not until we have demonstrated our persevering commitment to His will in this matter. Our act of persevering in controlling what we allow into our mind and what we dwell on in our heart is often the means that our faithful God uses to erase these offenses from our mind forever. Perseverance in this matter is the very mechanism of the maturation of our mind—the process of our sanctification.

It is normal for us to buy into this forgiveness plan with a little human reservation, with a plan to forgive everything except for one or two *special* offenses of hers. We must nevertheless remember that a forgiveness effort short of

Copyright 2005 Michael K. Pasque

perfection is an effort hopelessly doomed to failure. God wants us to forget every offense our wife has ever committed against us. Every one. We can't hold on to any of them. He wants us to be perfect in our forgiveness, just like He is perfect in His forgiveness.

Think I'm wrong on that one? We have to ask ourselves one little question. Are there any of our sins that we want God to not forget completely? Is there even a single one we would be willing to let Him remember? I don't think so. We want to be presented completely unblemished—washed white and pure by the blood of the Lamb—when we stand in His infinitely perfect, purely holy presence. Without the infinite perfection of His forgiveness, found only in the shed blood of Jesus Christ, we have no chance of standing before our infinitely pure God.

I don't know about you, but I'm going to try very hard to forget all of my wife's offenses. For despite my nailing His only Son to the cross of Calvary, God promises to forget *all* of my sins.

> *He will not always accuse, nor will he harbor his anger forever; he does not treat us as our sins deserve or repay us according to our iniquities. For as high as the heavens are above the earth, so great is his love for those who fear him; as far as the east is from the west, so far has he removed our transgressions from us.*
> —Psalm 103:9-12

> *"But if a wicked man turns away from all the sins he has committed and keeps all my decrees and does what is just and right, he will surely live; he will not die. <u>None of the offenses he has committed will be remembered against him.</u> Because of the righteous things he has done, he will live."*
> —Ezekiel 18:21-22 (emphasis added)

Notice that the permanent forgetting of our sins has to be a *willed* action on God's part. God can't forget because He's getting old or has Alzheimer's disease or something peculiarly human like that. He is not subject to forgetfulness like we are. He has to *actively* forget or it will not be forgotten. In most matters we do not need much help forgetting. But when it involves every one of our wife's offenses, we do. That is why this must also be an active willed process for us. The key to being perfectly successful at truly forgiving by truly forgetting is to recognize that we need God's help to do this. We have to ask Him for His help with the true intention of forgetting. We have to ask with the true belief in our hearts that we don't need to remember offenses.

Copyright 2005 Michael K. Pasque

God has already demonstrated His will to forget. He put His only Son on a wooden cross and let His Son's blood seal His memory loss. That is how badly He desired to forget our sins. That is exactly what He wants from us. He wants us to give Him our thoughts about our wife's offenses and let Him drive them out of our mind forever. He wants us to let Him cast them into hell where they originated, never to be dwelt upon again. But we have to ask Jesus from our heart every time. Once again, free choice—*we have to ask*. Only in His strength, the strength He showed on the cross, can we obtain victory over our intense, possessive desire to hold tightly onto our wife's offenses.

Our love for our wife must be as pure as God's love for the both of us. This is why our forgiveness must be perfect—complete, total and final. Pure love mandates pure forgiveness. Proving that point is why the perfectly pure God of all Creation had to go to the cross for us. This is tough stuff, this perfect forgiveness. It hurts. It hurts down in the deepest parts of our hearts. It mandates complete trust in God. This is because God doesn't put any conditions on our forgiving our wife, or anybody else for that matter. He just says *forgive*. We are to forgive in every circumstance because the Word of God never gives us any indication that we have any choice other than complete forgiveness in all circumstances. Jesus doesn't say, "forgive some men," He says, *"forgive men"* (Matthew 6:14-15). Nowhere in the written Word of God does it state that we are in any way to limit our forgiveness to a certain time or a certain type of person or, in fact, to refuse our forgiveness to anyone. Thank goodness He doesn't leave it up to us regarding when and whom we should and shouldn't forgive. In all of my worldly wisdom I have repeatedly wrecked every encounter where I have chosen to apply limitations or conditions to this command.

Further still, we really should never delude ourselves into thinking we can hold back in certain cases because *we by our great understanding of God's Word and purpose just know that this time our wife has crossed the non-forgiveness line.* This is a slippery slope indeed, this self-righteous belief that we somehow have been given *special* knowledge that allows us to discern that this time our wife is somehow undeserving of our forgiveness.

You, therefore, have no excuse, you who pass judgment on someone else, for at whatever point you judge the other, you are condemning yourself, because you who pass judgment do the same things. Now we know that God's judgment against those who do such things is based on truth. So when you, a mere man, pass judgment on them and yet do the same things, do you think you will escape God's judgment? Or do you show contempt for the riches of his kindness, tolerance and patience, not realizing that God's kindness leads you toward repentance?

—Romans 2:1-4

This little step onto the slippery slope of judgment always leads to more blindness and unsteadiness—which makes us want to put both feet on the slippery slope in the next *special* circumstance—and away we go. More blindness, more unforgiveness, more blindness, more unforgiveness—until we are never forgiving her *anytime*—and all of this, once again, in our great *wisdom*.

It really is much simpler to just do it God's way. We just forgive her *every* time in *every* circumstance. Then we don't have to spend time and effort trying to figure out when she deserves our very special forgiveness. We just forgive in every circumstance, no matter how bad, and we will be forgiven in every circumstance. Speaking from an eternal perspective, there is nothing more important than that.

For if you forgive men when they sin against you, your heavenly Father will also forgive you. But if you do not forgive men their sins, your Father will not forgive your sins.

—Matthew 6:14-15

Forgiveness is always possible. It is always an option. It is always *the* option. It is always the right thing to do in every circumstance. With it comes the unleashing of the power of God in our lives. What a story. It is engraved on the heart of every man—and it is time to quit ignoring it.

Jesus wants us to trust Him. We don't need to remember her offenses. Jesus will protect us if we will just trust Him and forgive her all of the time.

The world says, "That's naïve."

God says, "That's love."

Copyright 2005 Michael K. Pasque

Chapter 13

How Much Does Jesus Love Your Wife?

Assumption #13
Jesus died for your wife. He can't love her anymore than He already does. You must become like Jesus in your love for your wife.

You know that precious Savior that you seek to worship, serve, love, and glorify? You know that Awesome God whose face you desire to see continually? Remember that Lord of lords to whom you have given your heart and complete dominion over your life? Well…

He loves your wife!

He *really* loves your wife. Not only that, but he loves her all the time. He loves her even when she seems so unreasonable to you. He loves her when she is wrong. He loves her when she does something stupid. He loves her when she says something that is unbecoming of her walk with Him. He even loves her in the middle of that fight you just had with her. His love for her is unconditional. He loves her so much that He can't love her any more than He already does—and He will never love her less.

The next time you're having trouble forgiving your wife; the next time you can't find it in your heart to truly ask Jesus to help you forget every single one of her offenses toward you; the next time you just have to hold onto them so you can hold them against her in the future—remember this:

She was on His mind when He forced Himself up the winding steps to Calvary. He was looking her squarely in the face when the Roman soldiers pounded nails into His hands. The blood that dripped to the ground around that cross was shed specifically and most certainly for her.

Don't think for even a second that you can hold something against her. Even the God of all Creation has refused to hold any of her offenses against her! So exactly why do you think it is okay to even think about doing exactly that?

Difficult demands? You bet. But, as is always the case, Jesus doesn't just define the right course of action. He also serves as the only real source of the strength needed to carry it out. His cross is the solution and His cross is exactly where we get the strength to forgive. That is what the Gospel of Jesus Christ is all about. The cross of our Savior is the Fort Knox of love and forgiveness. Whenever you think you don't have any love or forgiveness for her, go there. Jesus has plenty, and He is always faithful to share.

> *The LORD is gracious and compassionate, slow to anger and rich in love.*
>
> —Psalm 145:8

Jesus knew we would be unable to handle this forgiveness thing if left to our own strength—so He already fought the forgiveness battle for us. This is critical since none of us, on our own, are capable of truly forgiving. Jesus is the source of *all* forgiveness. Every shred of forgiveness we can manage to muster is only by the victory of the battle He fought on the cross for us. So it should be no surprise that truly forgetting these offenses of hers always requires another trip back to the foot of His cross. It always requires another little trip down memory lane. Remembering exactly what has already been done for us makes it a lot easier to do the same for our wife. Remembering exactly how incredibly unworthy of His sacrifice, mercy, and saving grace we really are always puts us in the right frame of heart to forgive her. Forgiving and forgetting always requires another request for wisdom, strength, our own forgiveness, and His healing grace. The good news: God never gets tired of that request.

I would challenge you to pull closer to your Savior and try to peek over His shoulder at your wife. Look at her through His eyes. He absolutely loves her to death. Literally. His death. He went to the cross specifically for her—*specifically for her*. If she were the only person in all of history to accept the saving redemptive grace won on His cross that day, He still would have made the trip. He shed His blood and suffered separation from the Father just for her. It is—somehow—no less than exactly that personal. He loves her dearly. She is incredibly special to Him.

And that is who you are dealing with every day of your marriage—a woman who is cherished by the God of all creation. She is a daughter of the King. She is a crown princess of the eternal kingdom of God. Her desires, her tears, her feelings are precious to Him—and they should be precious to you. Next time you are the source of her tears, next time you are unhappy with her or thinking about holding something against her, ask Jesus for some of His love for her. He will always love her through your surrendered heart.

Copyright 2005 Michael K. Pasque

Chapter 14

Going Tactical

<u>Assumption #14</u>
The key to making it happen in your marriage is practice, practice, practice—perseverance every day, in every circumstance, every time.

We have discussed our *strategic* plan for interacting with our wife in a way that pleases God. Discussing a grand strategic plan is one thing, while actually implementing it on a day-to-day basis is another. The actual battles in this lifelong war are won or lost in the trenches, in our everyday interactions with our wife. We need a *tactical* battle plan, a plan that implements our overall strategic agenda in the battles of our everyday marriage interactions.

Honoring God in our marital relationship necessarily—by His precise design—means repeatedly making the correct moment-by-moment choices in the midst of the difficult life situations that we encounter with our life partner. It is in these very personal interactions with the people He brings into our life that we really get to know God personally. And this must be our goal: to know God wholly and personally every moment of our life.

The Word of God clearly teaches that knowing God through our interactions with those He places around us is a *process*. By His very design, it can never happen quickly. This is a problem for most of us. We live in a world of *quick fixes*. We are accustomed to demanding and getting quick solutions in everything we do. God's process for learning to obey Him in our daily personal interactions, however, is anything but quick. It is, in fact, a lifelong process. It will never be over until the moment we die. This is not negotiable; it is just the way this life of ours is masterfully designed.

This is where the challenge lies. As men, we are naturally project-oriented and just want to get our relationship with our wife *fixed* so we can move on. This is not going to happen here. This may be our plan—it certainly was mine—but clearly it is not God's plan.

Copyright 2005 Michael K. Pasque

This warfare that we find ourselves in, once again by God's precise design, is a battle of *perseverance*. We are persistently and repeatedly reminded of this in the Word of God.

> *Not only so, but we also rejoice in our sufferings, because we know that suffering produces perseverance; perseverance, character; and character, hope.*
> —Romans 5:3-4

> *Consider it pure joy, my brothers, whenever you face trials of many kinds, because you know that the testing of your faith develops perseverance. Perseverance must finish its work so that you may be mature and complete, not lacking anything.*
> —James 1:2-4

> *For this very reason, make every effort to add to your faith goodness; and to goodness, knowledge; and to knowledge, self-control; and to self-control, perseverance; and to perseverance, godliness; and to godliness, brotherly kindness; and to brotherly kindness, love.*
> —2 Peter 1:5-7

> *Therefore, among God's churches we boast about your perseverance and faith in all the persecutions and trials you are enduring.*
> —2 Thessalonians 1:4

> *I know your deeds, your hard work and your perseverance.*
> —Revelation 2:2

Winning this lifelong battle involves the complete transformation of our minds. It is indeed a victory of perseverance and is found only in actually changing the way we think every minute of every day of our lives. The transformation of our mind becomes the war of endurance that envelops us once we accept Jesus as the Commander of our hearts. The transformation of our mind by Jesus occurs only over many battles and is a war that is won only in the redeemed believer whose heart is surrendered to the King of kings.

> *Do not conform any longer to the pattern of this world, but be transformed by the renewing of your mind. Then you will be able to test and approve what God's will is—his good, pleasing and perfect will.*

Copyright 2005 Michael K. Pasque

—Romans 12:2 (emphasis added)

I don't know about you, but I had always believed that this transformation simply involved a thought process, something that just had to be *figured out*—a problem to solve, if you will. In other words, if I could just figure it out once and for all, then everything would be okay. "Sure," I thought, "once I just figure it out, it will all be different from that moment onward."

This is a typical *guy* attitude. In our minds, fixing our relationship with our wife should be like fixing the leak in the kitchen sink. You fix it. It's done. You move on. So, in the early years of my marriage, I spent all of my effort just trying to figure it out. The dilemma, as I am sure you have realized by now, is that even after you finally solve the problem, it is still incredibly difficult to continue to actually implement the solution on a day-to-day basis. There simply is no quick and sudden fix to the whole problem. Quite to the contrary, God has designed the system such that we must repeat the process over and over. This is the meat of the sanctification process. This is perseverance. As believers in the holy Name of Jesus, it is our destiny.

So how do we bear up under the requirement to repeatedly do it correctly, to persevere in our efforts to obey God's commands and decrees in our day-to-day married lives? To start with, we have to focus on reality. Not the reality we see around us, but the *real* reality. This reality tells us that this world and all the activities that we see going on around us are not what life is all about.

> *So we fix our eyes not on what is seen, but on what is unseen. For what is seen is temporary, but what is unseen is eternal.*
> —2Corinthians 4:18

The world and its prince would try to sell us on their version of reality. But surely life is all about God, not about the world we live in. We must, therefore, master a technique that immediately and consistently refocuses our minds on that fact alone each time we are faced with a relational challenge in our marriage.

This means we have to train ourselves to respond correctly in each situation. We have to respond reflexively in the correct manner, in God's way. This is in direct opposition to the reflex manner in which our sinful, worldly heart wants us to respond. The world's way of dealing with difficult interactions with our wife has been pounded into us all of our lives. It is the way we have been conditioned to respond. It is the *natural* way to respond.

It is also a dead end.

We have to learn a new response as part of the transformation of our mind. Then we have to learn to respond this way reflexively despite the persuasiveness of our years of exposure to the world and its version of reality. In this regard, we are like athletes. Most athletes want to be competitive at their sport. To do this, they must respond to the rapidly changing environment on the playing field with split second timing and in exactly the correct manner. The correct response, therefore, must be reflexive, automatic. There is only one way that athletes train themselves to respond in this manner: repetitive practice. Remember how hard you used to practice in high school sports just to be competitive? Is the goal of pleasing God any less deserving of our best effort than the goal of winning a Friday night football game?

Practice is what is needed, practice is what we are called to do, and practice is exactly what we will do. It all gets back to that *perseverance* issue we discussed before. Once again, we do not have a choice in this. Repetitively responding in the correct manner is one of the mechanisms God has chosen to mediate the transformation of our minds and our hearts into the mind and heart of Jesus Christ.

Practice is basically defined as simply repeatedly responding in the desired manner to a combat situation that is simulated on the training field. We are all well aware that Friday night football games are won by diligent practice the week before. It is the same for us as it is for athletes except that our practice occurs during our actual day-to-day living—*on the job training,* if you will. We have to come up with the correct reaction over and over again in real-life scenarios, in real-life battles.

So, how do we do that? The first step is a mandatory one. There is no reason to proceed any further if we haven't completed this first step. All is truly and eternally futile without it. As already alluded to, we must truly surrender our hearts to the sovereign Lordship of Jesus, the King of kings, in this and in every matter. He is King and Commander of the universe and desires to have that same position of absolute sovereignty in our hearts. Only when He has taken up permanent residence, permanent kingship in our hearts do we have any chance of responding correctly in the ambush situations that arise in our lives every day. Remember, *"out of the overflow of the heart the mouth speaks"* (Matthew 12:34). Only in the completely surrendered heart does our will become the same as His.

As we have discussed, the second step involves going directly to the written Word of God and training our mind on a daily basis to know exactly where God stands on each and every issue that can arise in our interactions with our wife. We have to know what God's direction is before we can even hope to make the right choice in the decisions we face with our wife each day. This cannot happen without a firm commitment to reading the Bible every day. It is as simple—and as complicated—as that.

The third step follows right on the heels of the second. Along with our dedicated reading of God's Word comes the need to go in supplicated prayer to

Copyright 2005 Michael K. Pasque

Jesus, the *Living* Word. Once the written Word of God has revealed what must be done, we still need to go to the only source of grace for the strength to actually do it. We can do nothing in regard to our sanctification without Jesus. We must go humbly to the foot of His cross and lay our sins and our lives and our crowns and our pride on the blood soaked dirt beneath it. Then we can ask Him to raise us up anew to face this daunting task of our transformation. By His design, we must do this every single day.

Only with daily nourishment on both the *Written* Word and the *Living* Word can we empower God's Spirit in our lives. Only with His Holy Spirit running our lives is any of this going to be possible. Without Him, we are already defeated. With Him, we are invincible. We need the Holy Spirit to remind us in every situation of the will of God for our lives. We need Jesus dead center in the middle of our hearts every single morning if we are to rely on the power of His cross to help us make the right choices. We go nowhere without taking these critical first steps.

This is why early morning time with the Lord has always been my preference and remains my very strongest recommendation. Early morning time spent in the Bible and on our knees before God is like warming up before a sporting event. It gets the clouds out of our mind and focuses us on the will of God in our life. Our mental muscles are loosened and warmed and able to focus on Jesus. This time together allows us to begin our day by thinking through some of the expected interactions we may have with our wife that day—especially during the difficult times. This doesn't take long at all, but can have a profound effect on how we respond later that day.

In my life, it is exactly in these early morning warm-up sessions that the Holy Spirit faithfully reveals the location and timing of the likely trouble spots I will face during the day. All I have to do is ask. There is no way we can know them all or even most of them. But we can anticipate many of them with the Holy Spirit's help. Then, we can begin thinking through and praying about the exact response that would please God in each of these situations. We can commit to Jesus that with His help we will respond in that exact manner when the time comes.

Then, after we have prepared, we can begin the day. As is always the case, we have to actually fight the battle. We can't just read about God's battle plan and seek His grace in its implementation. We have to actually step onto the battlefield. We have to fight the fight that is the transformation of our hearts and minds. And in this, we begin to train for eternity.

Copyright 2005 Michael K. Pasque

Chapter 15

This is a Test

Assumption # 15
Every time you feel anxiety in your relationship with your wife, it helps to remember: "This is a test."

Once we have prepared our minds in our morning warm-up sessions with Jesus, our goal must be to maintain the godly perspective that we have established by our reading of the Bible and supplication in prayer. Maintenance of this godly perspective is critical since only it will allow us to repeatedly respond correctly to the daily situations in which conflict arises with our spouse. What are the actual mechanics by which we can gain control over each of these situations and respond correctly to them the first time and every time? Our first goal must be to remove these occurrences from the emotional setting that surrounds them. If emotion is controlling the situation, we can be assured that we will not be viewing the whole matter with the correct perspective. Instead, we have to return godly objectivity to the scene by remembering that the Word of God assures us that in every marital encounter, *this is a test.*

This is a test.

This is not some random bad thing that just happened by chance to interrupt our day, to interrupt the harmony in our marriage. There is no random happenstance in this world. God knew before time began that He was going to be sending these situations right at us each day for His specific purpose in our life.

> *Remember how the LORD your God led you all the way in the desert these forty years, to humble you and to test you in order to know what was in your heart, whether or not you would keep his commands.*
> —Deuteronomy 8:2

God tests each of us with real life battle situations in order to *"know"* our heart. Actually, since He already knows our heart, He takes us through these tests to show *us* our heart; for it is our heart that God wishes to change. He can't change our heart unless we know our heart. This is because God won't change things without our permission. We have to recognize our sin first before we can ask Him to do what we cannot do, to free us from its grasp. God's necessary first step, therefore, is to use our sanctification partner, our wife, to reveal the deep-seated issues that no one except an intimate life partner can expose. Once they are exposed, our part is to acknowledge them, repent of them, and to ask Jesus to change them. Revealing our true heart to us is necessarily, therefore, God's first and continuing step in our sanctification—and our wife is critical to this process.

Each interaction with our wife must be viewed in this objective and eternal perspective. We must see things as God sees things, not as the world sees them. In this regard, there are no unimportant encounters on the battlefields of our relationship with our wife. We tend to discount the great majority of our daily interactions as being insignificant. They are, for the most part, handled in a naïvely casual manner. The truth, however, is that each and every interaction with our wife (and each and every interaction with every person we meet) is a test. God is always there. He is always asking the same question. He is wondering whether He is a high enough priority in our life at that exact instant for us to respond in a godly manner to the encounter He has sent our way. Each and every encounter is unique and nothing less than a once in a lifetime test sent by God. The pattern of God's testing is very consistent. Along with each new test situation comes two choices. In each case there really are only two possible answers: we can honor God by obedience to His commands or we can do things the world's way.

Until I let Jesus take control of my life, the world had controlled my every waking thought and was the basis for my every action. My habits were the world's habits; my thoughts, the world's thoughts; my responses, the world's responses. My actions were dictated totally by the world around me. The world had owned my mind for my entire life and *reality* was what I saw around me every day with no deference whatsoever to eternity. I lived every moment for myself and for the here and now. The world's view of my interactions with my wife—a perspective that had been hammered into my mind since our birth—is necessarily the polar opposite of the perspective that God has in mind. A complete transformation is precisely what is needed. This is why our sanctification is referred to as *"the renewing of [our] mind"* (Romans 12:2).

Satan and the world want us to downplay the importance of these encounters by getting us to think they are all just a result of random happenstance—not only did God not plan them, He doesn't even care about them. A casual attitude about them is the foot in the door that Satan needs to downplay the significance of our disobedience to God's will in each of these seemingly insignificant encounters. Minor, maybe. But they add up, and Satan knows it. The more we disobey God in the little things, the more the blindness builds up and the easier it is to completely miss the will of God in the big things.

Copyright 2005 Michael K. Pasque

Without a doubt, however, the more times I respond from the correct perspective by remembering that *this is a test,* the easier it gets. Perseverance and repetitive training is the key. We must repeat the correct response over and over. God keeps sending the tests and we keep choosing correctly. Pretty soon, our response becomes automatic. God's perspective becomes ingrained. God's will becomes our will. This is precisely our goal of goals. We want to know and be indwelled by the very heart and mind of Christ so that our response is automatic, with its only directing force being the will of God.

Repetition. That is the key. Just like football players repeat plays and drills over and over again, so do we have to repeat these little victories over and over again. Just like soldiers repeat battlefield tactics over and over again, so also do we have to persevere in repetition of the correct response in our interactions with our wife. Let there be no question about it, the big conflicts are coming. It is those conflicts that will make or break our relationship. But it is our responses in the little battles that prepare us for, and determine our response in, the critical situations.

For me, knowing that each occasion is a test changes everything. Knowing exactly this—that not only does my response matter to God, but that the whole thing has come about precisely because He sent it into my life—makes me want to pay close attention to every little detail. My goal is to honor and glorify Him in every single situation. Yours is too. Every opportunity missed is an opportunity missed for all eternity. These encounters matter, every one of them.

Our heart is the real battlefield and knowing the battlefield is the first step to going *tactical.* We have to know where our heart's priorities really lie. God wants to show us where we really place Him on our list of priorities. He brings every situation for exactly this reason. It is His good pleasure to test us, to know what is in our heart—to show us what is in our heart—by sending these challenging situations. Some are easy. Some are tough. All are meant to be revealing and instructive. The tough ones are also meant to humble us, to keep us away from that most heinous of sins, pride. It is our sin of pride that makes us think we can rely on our own efforts. It keeps us from relying on Him when change is needed.

It is precisely the knowledge that the difficult times with our wife are all tests that drives home another important point: *we are not the innocent victims of our wife's sin.* This is one of Satan's favorite lies. What an alluring pathway to anger and hate opens up to our weakened hearts when we believe it. Instead, we must remind ourselves that nothing sneaks past God. He would never allow the consequences of our wife's sin to affect us if it was not *His precise plan for our life.* It is a test. Getting angry with our wife and holding her sin against her is Satan's plan for our life. God wants us to face the true reality—that her sin in our life is a test sent by Him—and to respond to her with God's love and truth, not

Copyright 2005 Michael K. Pasque

with anger. If we are angry, we should get angry with God—not with our wife. Getting angry with God would, of course, surely be the most profound evidence of pride in our life. Humble submission to our wife—and to the will of God in our life—is the only intelligent, wise, realistic, efficient, and loving plan and it can only come from the correct perspective: *this is a test.*

God knows everything that is going to happen to us because He planned our every day. He has also promised us that the grace He supplies along with each of these tests is always enough to get us through it—if we will just stop and turn to Him, if we will just trust Him. It is in exactly this—turning to God in the middle of the fray—that we honor Him and bring glory to the Name that is above all names, Jesus. Then, with His strength, we can respond with the intellect and wisdom that is founded in His Holy Word rather than the emotional gut response the world would insist is our only way out. We can trust God, instead of trusting ourselves. He offers so much more than the false hopes offered by the world around us.

When we respond in a godly manner to the difficult tests we face every day in our marriage, we don't let emotions and pride elbow past the Holy Spirit. Instead of shoving Him out of the way in a vain human effort to save our old self-serving heart, we respond with the humility, servanthood, and love of the Savior who resides in our reborn heart. The more we do this, the easier it gets—it becomes automatic, reflexive. And this is the transformation of our mind and heart for which our wife has been waiting. For only then will she see the face of the One she seeks, in the man she calls her husband.

Copyright 2005 Michael K. Pasque

Chapter 16

What About the Kids?

Assumption # 16
You can't expect everything to be right with the kids unless things are right with their mother.

The Word of God clearly defines the nature of the complex interaction that exists between our relationship with Jesus and our relationships with the most significant people in our life—our wife and children. God has ordained a complex and holy interaction between these relationships that is always present and inviolate. This complex interaction has its foundation in a simple but critical fact: nothing has priority over our relationship with Jesus Christ. All else in our life, including our family, originates and derives meaning only in the defining light of this pivotal relationship. Our relationship with Jesus is the first and only real priority of our life. Very simply, God promises that if we seek Him first in everything we do, if we give Him unconditional kingship of our undivided heart, He will take care of everything else.

> *But seek **first** his kingdom and his righteousness, and **all** these things will be given to you as well.*
> —Matthew 6:33

As we have discussed, our relationship with our wife serves as a real-time barometer of our relationship with Jesus. If we are bowed in humble servanthood before our Lord, Creator and King, we will have no trouble assuming a servant's position with our wife. The same exact relationship exists with our children. If we are putting Jesus first in everything, He has promised—and is perfectly faithful—to take care of every detail of our life.

> *Trust in the LORD with all your heart and lean not on your own understanding; in all your ways acknowledge him, and he will make your paths straight.*
> —Proverbs 3:5-6

Copyright 2005 Michael K. Pasque

God's hand will therefore faithfully guide us through our relationship with our children if we place our trust in Him. But we can also take this one step further. God has also ordained a special interaction between our relationship with our wife and that with our children. *This holy interaction mirrors the interdependence of these relationships on our relationship with God.* In other words, our relationship with our children is directly dependent upon our relationship with their mother. Specifically, this means that we can have no chance of flourishing in our interactions with our children *without flourishing in our relationship with their mother*.

God has ordained a unique order of priority such that our Jesus-centered relationship with our children *goes through their mother*. First comes Jesus, then comes our wife, and then come the children. Just as we are to place Jesus first in every aspect of our relationship with our wife, so are we to place Him first in every aspect of our relationship with our children. But so also are we to place our wife first always in our relationship with our children. We must tend to our marriage relationship *first*. Just as our children's very lives emanated from that marriage relationship, so does our interaction with them. If our relationship with our wife isn't working, there is no chance that our relationship with her children will be working either. We can kid ourselves into thinking we can *get by* without first fixing our relationship with their mother, but it won't change reality. This is the God-ordained order of things and—like it or not—it always applies.

Think I'm wrong on this one? Let me ask you a question. What do you think our children would answer if we asked them how we could make our relationship with them better? There is no question about their answer. They would tell us to love their mother. They would tell us to make their mother happy and that would make them happy. Sure, we may be able to call to mind anecdotal instances that appear to represent exceptions to this rule. For the most part, however, these are only exceptions if viewed superficially. If heart-deep honesty is forthcoming, our children will always answer with their mother's interests at heart. They can't help it. It is written on their little hearts by the hand of Almighty God. They can deny it if they are in the middle of a little tiff with their mother, but deep down they know it is true. Such is the God-ordained relationship of mother and child.

Many men believe they can bypass this God-decreed order. They believe they can concentrate on playing ball with their son while their relationship with their wife is in a shambles. They think they can have long, meaningful discussions with their daughter while continuing to have knockdown, drag-out fights with her mother. It won't work. This does not mean we shouldn't play catch with our sons or have important discussions with our daughters. It just means we can't fool ourselves into believing that everything will be just great with our kids when we continue to raise our interests above those of our wife. This is not by my design

Copyright 2005 Michael K. Pasque

and certainly not by theirs. This is God's design and it is fact. Our children will never buy into our *truly* loving them when our actions show that we don't love the most important person in their young lives. This is not negotiable. Any attempt to subvert God's dominion over these relationships may—in our twisted, worldly logic—be commendable, but it is hopelessly bound to failure.

This is the bottom-line. If we get our relationship with Jesus in line, our perspective toward our wife changes. If we are living as a humbled servant of the Most High God, our relationship with our wife will be just fine—it can't help but be. This is what a truly humbled heart is all about. It then naturally follows that when we look up in the middle of all of this, as we run hard after Jesus and after our wife, we will realize that our relationship with our children is going just where God has planned. It may take a little while, but it will get there. One naturally follows the other. A good relationship with our kids extends quite predictably from the perspective that comes from humbling ourselves before our wife as God has decreed. It is the way God has set this life of ours in order. To ignore it sets our relationship with our family on unstable ground.

Now is the time to honestly and critically examine our hearts. We must ask ourselves the tough questions about our relationships with our wife and children. Are we still vainly embracing the misconception that we can continue to hold our wife's offenses against her, refuse to forgive her, and refuse to be a humble servant in our relationship with her? Do we still believe that our relationship with Jesus is completely separate from our troubled family relationships? Do we still believe that we can just concentrate on the kids and everything will be just fine as we wait for our wife to *come into line*? What do you think our children think about this attitude? Do you think for a second that they are going to let us get away with this? Once again, they can't. They can't because they are just responding to the inherent call of their hearts in the completely uninhibited fashion that characterizes children. They haven't learned to bury the cry of their tender hearts yet. They are just crying out from the most basic of the longings of their hearts: *they want their mother and father to love each other.*

They don't want just words to this effect. They want us to demonstrate this love by our actions. They want us to prevent the fights that distance us from our wife. They want a servant's heart to come to the rescue in response to the almost daily disagreements that naturally occur in a relationship between a man and a woman.

Our children's most important person is their mother. It is never going to be okay for us to mentally, verbally or physically abuse her, no matter how serious her offense. It will never be okay to run her into the ground, no matter how "stupid" she may seem or how "careless" her attitude toward things we think are important. We may think we have it all figured out. We may have constructed a complex rationale of why it is okay to do what we do to her. But, we must understand this: our children do not understand our rationale. They never will. They can't. They only want us to love their mother. The only kind of love their hearts understand is unconditional love. That is the love Jesus modeled and that is what our children expect. Nothing else will do.

Our children have seen first-hand the disastrous consequences of divorce acted out every day in their schools and neighborhoods. They interact on a daily basis with kids who get to see their fathers only every other weekend. They have seen the pain. They have seen the suffering and they, right this minute, are very, very afraid. They're afraid they're next. Every time we raise our voice in disagreement with our wife, it strikes a chord of terror in them that pierces deep into their worst nightmare.

Look into your children's eyes. The fear is there. Next time you and your wife start to travel down that pathway of non-servanthood that so often leads to an argument, stop and look at your children. Just stop, right in the middle of it all, and turn and look at them. No matter how old they are, they will be watching. No matter how hard you try to hide, their little eyes will be searching yours. They know their world and their wellbeing depends upon how these arguments end. They know their friends' families *seemed* to be doing just fine prior to the disastrous separation of *their* parents. Your children are afraid the same thing can happen to them. Just look into their eyes. You will see the fear. I have.

And when you look, if your children have instead just turned away, then it is you who should be afraid. If they are no longer even able to look at you when you carelessly let yourself be drawn into a fight with their mother, then you can be assured they are now running from what they fear. Things have gone on too long and they have gone too far. They have given up searching your eyes. They are no longer searching for the answer to the question on their hearts. They know the answer. Your actions have clearly told them. They are desperately afraid of what it might mean in their lives.

This is where you must step in. This is where you truly define your relationship to your family for all eternity. This is where the battle is either won or lost. This is where you either become the true leader of your family or forever lose this precious opportunity. This is where you are either a sheep…or the lion that God ordained you to be. This is *the* battle in the war to defend your family. You have to step in and you have to stop the warfare between you and your wife by humbling yourself before your God *and before her*. By God's design, there is no other way. Please be convinced. By God's decree there can be no other way.

Children pattern their whole lives after what they see during their childhood. They learn by example. They watch the important people in their lives to learn how to deal with the problems they will confront as adults. What are our daughters

Copyright 2005 Michael K. Pasque

learning from us when they observe our disagreements with our wife? Are they learning what an untrustworthy jerk a husband can be? Will they learn not to trust the man God has chosen for them? Will fear govern their every interaction with their husband? Will they learn to fear the fights like their mother fears them now?

Or do they see a man of God who knows God's heart in this issue? Do they see a man who is willing to be a humble servant to his wife? Do they see a man who places God's will and the wellbeing of his family above his pride? Do they see a man who can truly forgive? Do they see their mother being held up in a position of respect? Do they see a man leading his family by humbly serving them? Do they see their mother being completed by her husband, a man of God?

And what about our sons? Are they learning that mental, verbal and even physical abuse of a wife is the norm? Will they be using *us* as an excuse when they abuse their wife in a similar manner? Or are they learning that servanthood is the very heart of being a Christian husband? Are they learning to lead by being a servant? Are they learning to forgive? Are they learning that words matter little when godly actions don't back them up? Do they understand that their mother is our very special life partner and that we have the most extraordinary of relationships with her? Are they learning to be men of God from a man of God?

What is the greatest gift you can give your child? What gift will they remember for all time—for all eternity? What gift answers a too-often-unanswered cry from deep in their hearts?

Love their mother.

Serve her. Humble yourself before her in all circumstances. Lead her by being first in servanthood. *Love their mother.* Then in the environment of a family unified in the Holy Name of Jesus Christ, your children will come to know the Lord. They will take the step into eternity with you. They will become sons and daughters of the Living God. They will be ready for the sanctification process. They will have learned Christ's plan for *their* marriages and *their* families.

And your very first job as a father will be done.

Copyright 2005 Michael K. Pasque

Chapter 17

The Bottom-line

The bottom-line is simple. Our wife must come to know that no one less than Jesus Christ is at the center of our life and therefore at the center of our love for her. The centrality of Jesus Christ in our life and in our marriage is most palpably demonstrated by our subservient, sacrificial, loving leadership of our family. Our wife must come to know in her deep heart that the very foundation of our love for her, and therefore the very foundation of our marital relationship, lies exclusively in the One who rules over all creation—and over her heart.

All else is destined to fail.

By God's precise design, *all else is destined to fail*.

How can I be so sure about this? Simple. No matter how great we men think we are, the past tells another story. We lie, we fail, we are inconsistent, and we have proven by our actions that we cannot be trusted. These facts lie at the very heart of the overwhelming majority of marriage breakups. Men will be men—we can't help ourselves. We can never measure up to the expectations of our wife.

On the other hand, our wives all know—because it is written on their hearts—that in Jesus Christ they can always safely place their trust. He simply never fails. He is sovereign in everything, faithful always, and He has specifically told us that His infinite, unfathomable goodness directs His every move in our lives.

The key therefore, is to do everything in our power to shift the foundation of our relationship with our wife away from ourselves and toward faithful Jesus. He is the True North. He is our first priority. In exactly this fact is found the redemption of our marriage relationship. For He has promised that when we place Him first, *He will take care of everything else*. That is what every chapter of this book has been about. We must refer everything back to Him. We have to let His Holy Word be our only guide in our individual lives and in our marriages. As a married couple, we must take everything back to Him. We must give Him credit for every success in our families and take every failure to the hallowed ground at the foot of His cross.

You and I have a very important meeting coming up. It is the very next time that we see our wife. When we next see her, we are going to see her in a different light. We are going to see her in this new light for the rest of our life. We are never going to think of her except in this new light. For this new light comes from

Copyright 2005 Michael K. Pasque

viewing her through the eyes of Jesus in her proper perspective in our life. She is nothing less than that very woman chosen exactly and specifically for us by Almighty God. She is the very woman God chose to get us exactly where we, with every bit of our individuality intact, need to go to become more like His precious Son, Jesus.

Indeed, what a very high place in our life she holds and deserves as the woman chosen by God to spend her life with us. She is our special partner in the grand adventure He has planned. In a similar fashion, it is only as a co-warrior in this great adventure that she also can be fulfilled in our marriage relationship and truly know all that God has planned for *her*.

In her role as God's sounding board, chosen specifically with our sanctification in mind, our wife must be viewed as friend, not foe. Although Satan and the world will often attempt to paint her as the enemy, her God-designed, God-appointed role as a revealer of our deepest, most entrenched, most stealthy sin is absolutely invaluable to our sanctification. Whether we like it or not, and certainly whether we recognize it or not, we are not perfect. Not yet. And it is exactly in the attaining of that perfection—that becoming more like Jesus—that our wife's perfect role and God's perfect design for her in our life is most completely illuminated.

Our wife was not chosen for us only because of those characteristics we most singularly admire in her, those characteristics that drew us to her in the first place. Indeed, she was most specifically chosen for us because of the individual traits we hate so much. The things that drive us crazy are precisely the things that—if we can just stop and listen to what God is trying to tell us through her—will reveal our most deep-seated issues before the throne of God. These are problems that must be changed if we are to make progress in the transformation that God desires. We can be assured that precisely these issues are the most difficult ones for us to handle. They are the ones of which we are least aware. Our wife's contribution is critical to our quest to clear away all of the clutter of our life so that we may fully know and glorify God. For it is in the knowledge of God—a gift of grace from Him—that we are made into the likeness of Jesus. And then only in the likeness of Jesus can we bring glory to God.

We must therefore train our mind to look at our wife through God's eyes. We must remind ourselves of her key role in our life. We must remind ourselves that we simply cannot obtain all that God has planned for us without her. We must remind ourselves that every interaction with her is a test planned for us before time began. By nothing less than God's very precious decree, she holds a truly unique position in our life. Unlike all of the other men and women on earth, only she will know us at the very depth of our weakness when we choose to raise ourselves above her and our family. At the same time, only she will know the staggering

Copyright 2005 Michael K. Pasque

heights of our strength in Christ when we mirror the sacrifice of Jesus by humbling ourselves before her. She, very literally, is the only person who will know us at our very worst and at our very best.

God's call in our marriage is for us to love our wife for *all* that she is; not just as our lover and friend and confidante, but also for her God-designated role as the single person we will encounter in our whole life who will most represent Jesus to us. We must love her as we long to love Jesus. We must serve her as we long to serve Jesus. We must humble ourselves before her as we long to humble ourselves before our King. For in loving her, serving her, and humbling ourselves before her, we will in fact love, serve, and glorify Jesus. And that is expressly what we are all about.

> *May your fountain be blessed, and may you rejoice in the wife of your youth. A loving doe, a graceful deer—may her breasts satisfy you always, may you ever be captivated by her love.*
>
> —Proverbs 5:18-19

www.ingramcontent.com/pod-product-compliance
Lightning Source LLC
Chambersburg PA
CBHW060652030426
42337CB00017B/2578